Praise for Life's Accessories

~∾⌒

"In Rachel Levy Lesser's episodic memoir, worn talismans give her the strength to claim her voice, weather grief, and navigate a rich and full life. With writing reminiscent of Ilene Beckerman's classic *Love, Loss, and What I Wore*, Lesser captures the pressures and pleasures of a new generation of women as her warmth and wisdom shine through."

—ANDREA JARRELL, author of *I'm the One Who Got Away: A Memoir*

"*Life's Accessories* is a poignant story told through the universal language of stuff. Rachel uses meaningful items from her past to weave together stories that made her into the wife, mother, and daughter she is today. From perms to summer camp, post-baby weight loss to making mom friends, Rachel paints a relatable, compelling picture of her highs and lows, and beautifully writes about the loss of her mother. *Life's Accessories* is this season's must-have accessory for your best girlfriend's bedside table."

—ZIBBY OWENS, writer and creator/host of the podcast *Moms Don't Have Time to Read Books*

"I literally could not put this book down. I fell in love with Rachel on page one, and by the last chapter I was convinced she was my long lost BFF. She writes with humor and grace, and takes us on her life's journey with vulnerability and wit. It's a winning combo! Rachel is as real and authentic as it comes. Wish we could be mom friends in real life!"

—ALI KATZ, author of *One Minute to Zen*

"*Life's Accessories* is a charming and deeply relatable exploration of the power inanimate objects—clothing and accessories—have to remind us of who we are and of where we came from. Lesser imbues each anecdote, centered on a piece of clothing, jewelry, or accessory, with humor, wisdom, and memory. She excavates her own personal history through particular objects in her closet, and makes the personal universal. I laughed, I cried, I nodded vigorously in agreement as I read. I loved this book."

—LINDSEY MEAD, writer and editor of *On Being 40(ish)*

"Often our memories of those we have lost are mere glimpses and images of the past and our time with that person. In *Life's Accessories*, Rachel Levy Lesser honors us with the privilege of those glimpses and images through the beautiful window of her words. You will laugh, cry, and sit with the words of wisdom that Rachel shares. Her gift of storytelling will find you reflecting on the accessories you carry with the memories of those you have loved and lost."

—DARCY WALKER KRAUSE, Director, Uplift Center for Grieving Children

"*Life's Accessories* cleverly uses articles of clothing and jewelry to shape the story of the author's life. Lesser's stories are relatable and accessible. Reading her memoir is like sifting through a closet with a friend, stopping to pause over certain items and remembering why they meant so much in the first place. She artfully reminds us how even just thinking about an object can immediately transport us right back to a moment in time."

—BETH RICANATI, physician and author of
Braided: A Journey of a Thousand Challahs

"A thoroughly enjoyable read from an author who immediately feels like your best friend as she grabs your arm and reveals stories equally lighthearted and tender about motherhood, family, love, loss, and friendship."

—MARISA BARDACH RAMEL, author of
The Goodbye Diaries: A Mother-Daughter Memoir

"In fluid, engaging prose, Rachel Levy Lesser draws readers into her episodic coming-of-age story, from prep school student to mature mother and writer—accessorized charmingly throughout by symbolic talismans. Though grieving for her lost mother, she exudes a palpable joie de vivre, attracting a lively coterie, including us who read, as Best Friends Forever."

—PAULA DEITZ, editor of *The Hudson Review*

Life's Accessories

Life's
Accessories

a memoir
and
fashion
guide

RACHEL LEVY LESSER

SHE WRITES PRESS

Published 2019
Printed in the United States of America
ISBN: 978-1-63152-622-0
ISBN:. 978-1-63152-623-7
Library of Congress Control Number: 2019906554

For information, address:
She Writes Press
1569 Solano Ave #546
Berkeley, CA 94707

Interior design by Tabitha Lahr

She Writes Press is a division of SparkPoint Studio, LLC.

For Neil. I've loved growing together with you.

Contents

~∿

Signet Ring Sans Family Crest

Eighth grade really sucked. I know it probably sucked a little bit for a lot of people, but I'm going to say for me, it sucked more. I was perfectly content in my seventh-grade existence at my little Quaker school, Newtown Friends School, in suburban Philadelphia. I had been at the little school since kindergarten. When my mother's friends asked her about her decision to send her two Jewish kids to a Quaker school in the farmlands part of suburban Philadelphia, she used to say, "They just feel good about themselves when they go to school every day."

Although this sounded super Kumbaya-ish and maybe a bit hard to believe, it was true. I liked going to Newtown Friends School. I did feel good about myself and comfortable in my own skin there. The school was so small that you had to be friends with everyone in your grade, and they had to be friends with you too. As the song goes (kind of), I don't know much about history or biology or the French I took, but I do know that I was happy—until eighth grade, that is.

My father, uncle, brother, and older cousins had all attended the Lawrenceville School, a traditional all-boys prep school in New Jersey, just five miles down the road from Princeton University. Lawrenceville was exactly like you'd imagine any school called the [insert name of East Coast small town] School would be. It was *Dead Poets Society*, *A Separate Peace*, and *School Ties* all wrapped into one. Lawrenceville broke its 177-year-old tradition of accepting only boys in 1987, which just happened to be the year I was entering eighth grade.

I don't remember the application process. I don't remember a conversation with my parents about whether I should stay or leave my small, utopian Quaker school for the big, unknown prep school. I just remember feeling like an alien from the very first day I stepped onto Lawrenceville's campus. All of the other newly admitted girls looked alike and appeared to know what they were doing. They had been prepped for prep school. Most of them had blond hair, all of them had straight hair, and they wore long skirts from Laura Ashley and turtlenecks from J.Crew every day to class. A decent percentage of them went by nicknamed versions of Elizabeth, Katherine, or Mary—lots of Lizzies, Kates, and Mollys, and also a few Betsys, Kats, and Mimis. The boys had names like Hunter, Trevor, and Tripp. The Tripps were actually triples, as in the IIIs, as in Thurston Howell the third.

This is the part where my husband, Neil, who had never

met anyone who went to prep school until he met me, rolls his eyes and plays his air violin for me. He calls me a pioneer in the world of coeducation at elite private schools. I get it. I really do. I fully appreciate the fact that I was born in the late twentieth century into a free, wealthy country complete with free speech, equal rights, and clean water and air. I had parents who gave me food, clothing, shelter, unconditional love, a top-notch education, and amazing opportunities—not to mention second-to-none emotional support and stability. I am appreciative. I am grateful.

Everyone I knew loved my parents. Becky and Jimmy Levy were adorable. Their matching blue eyes, freckled faces, and light brown (until my father went prematurely gray in his early forties) hair often confused people, who thought they were brother and sister. After hearing that a few too many times and wanting to throw up in my mouth just a little bit, I could see it, too. They held hands in private and in public. Jimmy referred to Becky as his girlfriend, as in telling the waitress at the burger joint in town, "I'll have what my girlfriend's having." Becky winked at the waitress, but not in a creepy way. She winked at most everyone, and she got away with it. That's how adorable she was.

At a time when most kids wanted to get away from their parents, I found myself wanting to be with mine more. Neil finds this perplexing. I cried after my father set up my computer on my desk in my college dorm room and my mother finished making my bed, because I knew they would be leaving me soon. I suspected that my parents were cooler than I was and that they had their shit together more than I imagined I ever could. They seemed to have all the answers. And so I trusted them implicitly, even back in eighth grade, when I was pissed at them for uprooting my life.

My mother would later say that I loved being at the prep school (100 percent not true), and my father would say he thought I should have stayed at the Quaker school (also 100 percent not true). Revisionist history played well in my childhood house.

The majority of the students at the prep school were boarders. The girls I observed/studied/wanted to be like had quite easily left their friends and families behind at ages fourteen and fifteen to share a dorm room with another girl named Kate or Molly, whose Laura Ashley quilt matched not only the first girl's own quilt but also her jewelry box and her vast collection of flowered prairie skirts.

I was a day student (read: freakish townie girl), which was a blessing and a curse. My parents would never have let me live at school, and I really didn't want to. But still I began to understand fairly quickly that I would miss out on probably the most important part of prep school life by going home every afternoon. My day-student/visitor status did not stop me from trying to blend in with the other students, whose lives looked just about as beautiful and perfect as the man-icured green lawns and mature trees surrounding the dorm rooms and classroom buildings. The Lawrenceville campus, which was designed by the same architect who planned Central Park, rivaled most college campuses with its stately redbrick halls, old stone chapel, ice hockey rink, golf course, and squash courts.

In a cruel twist of fate, eighth grade was also the year my mother let me get a perm. I had begged her for years to let me put into my lifeless, pin-straight hair whatever chemicals would add some curl and volume. She was pretty strict, insisting that my straight hair was "so pretty and classic" and asking why I would "want to mess that up." I can't answer that question now. I guess I thought messing up my classically straight and—though I failed to notice it at the time—preppy hair would give me some kind of confidence to help me adjust to the trauma that was eighth grade. Or maybe the perm was an unconscious way for me to inflict pain on myself—the late-1980s version of teenage cutting? I guess my mother sensed my pain, and so she gave in to the perm. She shouldn't have.

I cried the whole way home from the salon as I sat in the back seat and my mother and older brother, Jonny, glanced at me from the comfort of the front seat and their own natural straight heads of unpermed hair. They told me my hair didn't look that bad, but they were terrible liars. I took a shower the minute I walked into my house, doing whatever I could to wash the frizz masked as curls out of my formerly classic, preppy, pin-straight hair. Three rounds of vigorous shampoo scrubs helped a little, but I had other challenges to deal with. My mother's hairdresser, a man named Michel with a questionable French accent, had cut layers into my hair to make the perm take shape. I looked like a teenage Farrah Fawcett (minus the gorgeous face and unbelievable body) who had just stuck her finger in an electric socket.

My new look didn't give off the new, cool-girl vibe I was going for. The layered, half-washed-out frizzy hair only exacerbated the whole *you're too tall, too freckly, too dark haired, one of these things is not like the other* vibe I was sensing from the adorable, blond-bobbed, button-nosed teenage prep school girls. The girls were not mean to me, but they also didn't embrace me, and I can't really blame them. I didn't like eighth-grade me then, and I cringe when I think about her now.

In my own version of a Julia Roberts *Pretty Woman* makeover, I decided that I would do whatever it took to become, or at least look like, the all-too-cute-and-together girls at school. I dragged my mother with me to the preppy shops in Princeton, where she said yes to just about every Laura Ashley long skirt and J.Crew cable-knit sweater, and even a pair of Sebago penny loafers. I put real pennies in the loafers and wore them without socks, even in the winter. I give my mom a lot of credit for giving in to my fourteen-year-old whims to prep-school-girl myself up. I sensed she knew this look, this dressing up as someone else, was not the greatest idea, but she was willing to do what it took to bring her teenage daughter some joy—to help her fit in. I would have done the same for my own kid.

Years later, when I started to get my shit together as a young adult, my mother told me that it broke her heart to watch me walk down the stairs, into our yellow country kitchen, every morning for breakfast before school, looking more and more like a Kate or a Betsy and less and less like myself. That broke my heart a little to hear.

"This hurts me more than it hurts you," my mother said when I called her from the pay phone in the hallway of the eighth- and ninth-grade girls' dorm, asking if she could pick me up early from school because, I said, "I have no friends." I wish I could take that thirty-year-old dagger out of her heart.

I can only imagine how I would feel if my tween daughter uttered those words to me today.

I asked my parents for a signet ring for my birthday in eighth grade. Several of the very popular Mollys, Courtneys, and Lizzies had signet rings. Their rings were legitimate, as in they were real, solid gold, had their own family crest or great-grandfather's initials on them, and had been passed down to them from generations dating back to the *Mayflower*, I guess. In some cases, and I learned this from watching old British movies, the initialed imprint on the signet ring was dipped in ink and used to sign and seal official royal family documents. I bet those girls had royal blood in them.

My mother drove me to the jewelry store in town one day after school to help me select a modern-day, first-generation, Jewish-girl version of my own. "Rach wants a signet ring," she said to her friend, also the jewelry store's owner. I'm pretty sure she winked at him in a nonverbal effort to say, *Yes, I am buying my fourteen-year-old Jewish daughter a piece of jewelry designed for old English kings, and no, I am not crazy. I am just doing what it takes to make my miserable, awkward teenage daughter smile and feel good about herself, even for just a moment.*

We selected a small, gold-plated (not even close to solid) ring with a round face and asked for my initials—RAL—to be engraved on the face. I'm trying to think of an equivalent gift I could buy for my daughter today. A pony? A tiara?

I wore the signet ring through all five years of prep school as I dressed in costume every day, playing (quite well, I must say) the role of the preppy prep-school girl. The perm grew out. The sweaters, turtlenecks, and long skirts began to look more natural on me. I wore the pearls that my grandmother had given me for my bat mitzvah hanging out over my turtleneck every day. I borrowed Jonny's bar mitzvah blue blazer and on occasion wore it over the turtleneck. My mom found her old wool toggle coat from college in our attic. I dusted it off and wore it over the turtlenecks, sweaters, and long skirts when it got really cold.

Neil very correctly called me out as a chameleon one night in 2013 when I got dressed up to attend a holiday dinner party for his office.

"Who are you?" he asked, as I walked down my grown-up house steps wearing a gray wool pencil skirt, a red silk blouse, and pearls—the same ones from my bat mitzvah.

"I'm the partner's wife tonight," I replied, explaining to him how I could be anything he or anyone else ever needed me to be, but not in a smutty way, of course. Neil smiled, knowing full well what I meant. I looked almost unrecognizable from the person I normally dress as: a writer-yogi-boho mom, which is actually who I am. On the night of the dinner, however, I knew that I needed to play a role, and in order to do so, I had to dress the part. I'm really good at that. I can dress up as a power-suited, corporate MBA; a workout-clothes-and-hoodie-wearing stay-at-home mom; a high-fashion lady who lunches; a no-frills-no-makeup volunteer; and, I bet, a few other people were I given the challenge.

Having watched way too many episodes of *Oprah* after class in college and graduate school, I really do know who my true, authentic self is (see writer-yogi-boho mom), but I also know that sometimes, even if for only one evening, I may need to dress up/play the role of someone else. I think Oprah would be okay with that. I've seen her do it herself.

I take pride in being able to become whoever I need to be in order to blend in, to make others around me feel comfortable. I learned how to do this from the very best—my mom. She put everyone around her at ease, including her children, her husband, her friends, her children's friends, the students she taught in elementary and nursery school, and even the lady at the Wawa who rang up her decaf every morning when she went out for coffee long before going out for coffee was a thing.

"She was my favorite grown-up," said my awesome childhood friend for life, Stacey, about my mom to me one day when we were discussing the people we loved, hated, and were scared shitless of when we were kids. I understood why.

"I wore a signet ring for five years in high school," I said to Neil as we walked out the door that night to the work dinner. He shook his head, looking mostly amused and only slightly perplexed, which is a look he has given me on many occasions.

I could have been cast in a John Hughes movie back in eighth grade—the one about the awkward townie girl from the other side of the tracks who becomes one of the preppy, popular girls, then makes one real friend and discovers she doesn't need to pretend to be like anyone else anymore. I was exactly like that girl in that movie, only there were no tracks or other side of them in my town, and I never became all that popular. The part about my finding the one true friend is true.

Her name was Amanda. She blended in with the popular girls, but I could tell she was different. Amanda was tall, like I was, and had brown hair, even slightly darker than mine.

She was way more prepped for prep school life than I was, having grown up on prep school campuses and lived in faculty houses with her brothers, her mother, and her father, who was a prep school English teacher. Amanda was so funny and even more fun to be around, and we shared many interests, none of which included watching the Tripps and Trevors play lacrosse.

Amanda boarded at school, as her family lived on the campus of another prep school in New England. She had strong ties to Lawrenceville, though, since her father had taught there when Amanda was younger. A lot of the teachers and teachers' spouses who lived on campus knew Amanda really well. They always gave her a big greeting when she walked by them on campus, and in time they gave me those same friendly greetings as I walked next to her. We became known as a little twosome on campus, almost always walking together in between classes and on our way to and from the dining hall. I loved it when the teachers stopped to talk to us.

Amanda later told me that she loved it when Jonny, who was just a year ahead of us at Lawrenceville (and a known figure on campus because of his famous overly gregarious nature and his legitimate school leader status as editor of the school's weekly newspaper), would yell to us across campus "love you, pals" and "make a great day." Jonny adopted those statements from my father, who said something like that to Jonny and me every morning as we headed out the side kitchen door on our way to school. These across-the-campus very public displays of affection embarrassed me but also made me feel a little bit special. And when Amanda yelled back "we love you too, pal Jonny," I had to laugh.

Amanda brought me along with her to her Friday-night babysitting jobs at our favorite teachers' houses. I brought her back to my house for Saturday-night sleepovers. We baked cookies, went to the movies, and shopped for turtlenecks and sweaters. We laughed—a lot.

Amanda's parents got divorced in tenth grade. It got bad. I marveled at the way she carried herself through her parents' split. I could barely handle a perm; Amanda kept smiling and laughing, and even though she was going through way more shit than I could ever have imagined back then, I still felt like she was the leader of our little pack of just us two. She would later tell me that spending the weekends at my house with me and my parents (this confirmed my hunch that my friends thought my parents were cooler than I ever was) got her through the insanity of living away from home with all the Kates and Kats as her own home life was becoming undone.

Amanda and I are still close. We kept in touch through college, even visiting each other in Florence and London when we studied there during our junior year. After college, Amanda served in the Peace Corps in Namibia, which apparently is where the hard-core Peace Corps members go. For two and a half years, she lived in a tiny African village where she peed and pooped in a hole in the ground and taught English to African children. Are you getting this? She's a quality person. She's awesome. I'm lucky I found her in the sea of Kates and Kats that was prep school.

Amanda wrote me a letter from her tiny African village right before I got married. She told me about life without running water in Namibia, about her students, and about how sad she was not to be able to make it back stateside for my wedding.

"You were the only reason I got through high school," she wrote.

I shook my head in disagreement. *She* was the reason *I* got through it.

The Gray-Team Captain Necklace

and the Greatest Honor of My Life

I can divide just about every population I find myself in into two categories: those who went to sleepaway camp and those who did not. Let's start with the latter. Those who did not go to sleepaway camp, or have never heard of it, think that the concept is insane. I get it. If I hadn't gone and loved it so much that I made Neil promise above all else that if we had children one day, we would send them to sleepaway camp, I would probably think it was insane, too.

People who did not go to sleepaway camp can't understand why seemingly smart, capable, loving, involved parents would shell out thousands of dollars to send their children, starting when they are as young as seven or eight, to live in rickety old cabins in the woods, far away from the comforts of home, for seven weeks every summer. They can't wrap their heads around the cold lake swims, the institutional, unhealthy food, the lack of electronics or contact with the outside world, and being away from their kids for so long.

I am in the former part of that population—those of us who went to sleepaway camp and, furthermore, loved it. I believe it was far and away the best gift (besides life, of course) that my parents gave to me, and I feel equally lucky that I am able to give this gift to my children.

I went to Camp Tapawingo for the eight best summers of my life, beginning in 1983. *Tapawingo* is a Native American word (in 1983 we called it an Indian word) meaning "place of joy." That is what it felt like for me and the other, mostly Northeastern, mostly Jewish girls who spent our childhood summer days swimming in the freezing, scary, mushy-on-the-bottom lake and playing tennis on the well-kept Har-Tru courts, which had a perfect view of the cold, scary lake. We participated in every campy sport imaginable, including soccer, basketball, archery, softball, lacrosse, and my favorite, Newcomb, which is just volleyball for uncoordinated people. I excelled at Newcomb.

Camp for me was more than just playing sports during the day and sleeping in a cabin in the woods at night. It was a place where I grew into myself and in many ways discovered who I was. It was a place where, far from the pressures of home and of school, I formed lifelong friendships with other girls whom I trusted and grew to love like I never quite could with the kids at home. It was also where I learned how to do things that I never could have done at home—like climb a mountain, water-ski, write a song, and lead the gray team against the blue team in my last summer as color-war captain. At camp I learned to truly appreciate the simpler things in life: friendship, natural beauty, the outdoors, tradition, and teamwork.

I counted down the long winter days on my Camp Tapawingo wall calendar, which hung above and exactly in between my two twin beds in my childhood bedroom, until at long last June arrived. I couldn't wait to leave my real-world life behind and travel by plane to Boston and then by bus to Sweden, Maine, to my second home, where I would live among the pine trees that swayed in the summer breeze and so too the rippling waves that slipped by canoes with ease. Those are words from a camp song. I am not that poetic.

At camp, we sang songs all the time. No one cared if you couldn't carry a tune. No one cared if you sucked at sports or at arts and crafts—although (full disclosure) I never knew anyone who really sucked at arts and crafts. No one cared what you looked like at camp. You walked around all summer in your camp uniform, with no makeup and with your usually wet-from-the-lake hair thrown back in a ponytail or a braid. I can still recall that feeling of the fresh Maine air on my face and the late-afternoon summer sun on my back as I hiked up the big camp hill, past the flagpole, to the dining hall while holding hands in a giant chain with my camp besties. I've actually channeled this thirty-plus-year-old feeling of pure, simple childhood joy while dealing with real grown-up challenges and real grown-up life crap. It works. It helps.

I'm pretty sure I daydream about the seemingly mundane, away-from-the-comforts-of-home stuff we used to do at camp way more than a high-functioning adult human being should. During rest hour after lunch and again right before lights-out at night, we played card games like spit and war, old maid and gin. We traded stickers and stationery and gambled for gum in heated rounds of blackjack. We played jacks, braided each other's hair, and told long-winded stories that seemed funnier and way more interesting at camp than they ever did at home.

If camp sounds a bit like a cult, it's because it was. It still is. I imagine cabin life at an all-girls sleepaway camp to be somewhat like life for the mole girls down in the bunker—obviously without all the violent, evil, and super-crazy stuff. The most cultlike behavior one learns at sleepaway camp comes straight out of color war. I bet the camper part of the population is nodding their heads right now. Not sure what the other part is doing.

Color war is the sacred time of the summer, usually during the last week or two—or, in the case of Camp Tapawingo, the entire eight (now seven) weeks—of camp, where the whole camp is divided up into two teams, each named for a different color, and children compete against each other with a warlike mentality in just about every activity imaginable. There are competitions in sports, on land, and in the lake; in song; in fire starting and in rope burning; in staying silent during meals; and in blowing the biggest bubbles with the gum that parents back home send. It's 100 percent cultlike, and it's 100 percent awesome. I get nervous thinking about it even now, as I chant color-war cheers in my head for the gray teams of the past, present, and future.

Each color-war team has a captain—a team leader who

fights valiantly, with every fiber of her being, to win. The team captain is like a queen, a president, and a community organizer all rolled into one teenage, mostly Northeastern, mostly Jewish girl who swears her allegiance to each member of her team for life. In some camps, the captains are chosen in a democratic and free all-camp election. At other camps, the camp directors and head counselors handpick the captains. In case you haven't figured it out yet, being a color-war captain is a big fucking deal.

I can't remember what I ate for breakfast yesterday, but I can tell you without hesitation the names of the gray-team color-war captains from all eight of my summers at Camp Tapawingo: Tammy Kafin, Caroline Tulenko, Tracy Kramer, Abby Miller, Debbie Bindeman, Alison Forman, Jessica Cohn, and, in my final summer, me—Rachel Levy.

In 2017, my grown-up mom friend Randi was at a family friend's bat mitzvah when she ran into a woman whom she knew from growing up and who, coincidentally, had gone to camp with me. As they caught up on their lives since childhood, playing a strong version of the name game, they realized that they both knew me. Randi relayed their catch-up conversation to me, which went something like this:

Grown-Up Camp Friend: "You do know that Rachel was a really big deal at camp. She was the captain of the gray team."

Randi: Smiling and nodding, with the following thought bubble above her head: *Wow. That must have been a big deal when you were twelve, but we're adults now, so get over it, you batshit-crazy lady.*

Grown-Up Camp Friend clearly couldn't get over it. I can't get over it. Those of us in the population who went to camp and drank the Kool-Aid (it was actually bug juice) can't get over it, either.

My awesome friend for life Lauren, whom I met in college, illustrated this very point during our sophomore year in another cultlike setting: sorority rush. Lauren sat among her Tri Delta sisters in an old, oversize lecture room in Steinberg–Deitrich Hall at the University of Pennsylvania as the girls worked late into the night, faced with the task of selecting their new pledge class—their new sisters.

I was also in a sorority in college. I had the sorority pin, once wore a toga, and knew the secret handshake, but when I look back on sisterhood now, I find the whole situation quite bizarre. Greek life can be a good way for kids to make friends while away at school, especially at the big schools. But as a parent of kids who will be starting college in just a handful of years, I feel a little nauseated when I think about other kids deciding if my kids are good enough to hang out with them. Plus, the whole hazing thing freaks me out in a way I just couldn't see back when I was younger.

I will give props to the Panhellenic rush system at Penn, in that I owe my marriage and my children's very existence to it. I met Kara, another awesome college friend for life, on the porch of our sorority house during rush, and we became sisters and friends because some upperclassman chicks in one sorority liked us and some other upperclassman chicks in another one apparently didn't like us. I doubt I would ever have met Kara in college without becoming her sister, as I lived in the tiny loser freshman dorm next to the law school library. Kara lived in the quad, which was where anyone who ever went to Penn or anyone who ever knew anything about where people lived at Penn lived. After graduation, while living and working in New York City, Kara introduced me to her boyfriend's best friend from growing up. That was Neil. Thanks, sisterhood.

The Tri Delta sisters were having trouble deciding whether one particular freshman girl should be granted sisterhood status and allowed to wear the oversize Champion brand sweatshirt with the three delta triangles on it. Yes, this was a ridiculously organized and somewhat cruel process, but a process nonetheless. Hoping to put an end to the seemingly endless enterprise and to the meeting altogether, Lauren raised her hand to speak.

"Um, I went to camp with Kim, and she was the captain of the white team," said Lauren, quite satisfied that she had proven her point.

Half of the sisters took in this valuable information, writing it down, some underlining "captain of the white team" in their college ruled notebooks, including another one of my awesome college friends for life, Penny, a camper, albeit an unhappy one, in her own right. The other half stared at Lauren and then began asking each other, in soft, confused voices, "What the fuck is she talking about?" The note-taking sisters had gone to camp. The staring, soft-talking sisters had not. The note-taking sisters knew instinctively that the color-war team captain was a girl they wanted in their sorority. Furthermore, they knew that if word about Kim's white-team captain status got out to the other sororities, they would want her, too. After a twenty-minute discussion on the leadership and key life skills that a camp color-war team captain must possess, the sisters decided to make Kim a Tri Delta sister.

Camp Tapawingo rewarded each of its own team captains with a super-thin, super-fake silver disk that hung on the end of an equally super-fake silver chain. These tokens of appreciation for camp leaders were given out at the big banquet on the last night of camp. Banquet is a really fun night and also a really sad night, as campers try to hold on to a few more hours of their precious summer, knowing full well they'll be traveling back into their non–place of joy real world the following morning. The camp banquet has the bittersweet vibe of the big end-of-summer party in *Dirty Dancing*—the one where Patrick Swayze tells Jerry Orbach, "Nobody puts Baby in the corner" and then takes her to the stage, where he slowly runs his hand down her arm and they dance flawlessly together to "(I've Had) The Time of My Life." It's like that, minus Patrick Swayze, Jennifer Grey, and an awesome soundtrack.

I accepted my gray-team captain necklace on banquet night, beaming with pride as I stood next to my best friend and awesome friend for life from camp Liza while she was awarded the blue-team captain necklace. Somehow our friendship survived the intense color-war rivalry. I still have my necklace. I still call Liza my best friend from camp. I still introduce her to others with that auspicious title. I wore the gray-team captain necklace almost every day for the next two years, until I went to college. Yes, that math is correct: I went to camp until I was sixteen.

My gray-team captain necklace has seen better days. It's tarnished and scratched, and I don't know what happened to the chain part. I keep it in my jewelry box on top of my dresser and catch a glimpse of it on a fairly regular basis as I search through the oversize box for bangle bracelets or a long, tasseled necklace to go with my current writer-yogi-bo-ho-mom look. When I see the gray-team necklace, I think of the great summer of 1990. That summer seems like a million years ago, in a place only those who lived it with me could ever really understand. That small, thin piece of tin reminds me of what it felt like to have found my place in my own little piece of the world for the very first time. It reminds me of the great sense of self, of honor, of responsibility that came with color-war team captain status.

I wrote my college essay about being the gray-team captain. I can't believe I did that. I can't believe I got into college with that essay. I bet college applicants today write about building robots, constructing houses in third-world countries, and curing cancer.

Last summer, I was listening to a *This American Life* podcast from NPR as I drove home from the grocery store in my giant SUV, which seemed extra giant with my kids, away at camp in their own places of joy, not in it. This particular podcast was titled "Notes on Camp" and featured stories from people of all ages around the country who had experienced the joys, the challenges, the memories, and the magic of camp.

A grown woman named Dana Harden, who was interviewed for the show, explained how she still gets teary all these years later, thinking about having been named color-war captain in her last summer at her camp, so many years ago.

"It was the greatest honor of my life," she said, her voice shaking just a bit. I nodded my head vigorously in agreement as I drove along and felt a tear roll down my cheek. It was for me, too.

Elsa Peretti Every Day

I admire those people who wear one very special piece of jewelry every day—that one piece that is so meaningful to them, they could never imagine taking it off. I think this stems from my childhood infatuation with Little Orphan Annie and the broken-heart locket her parents gave her as a promise that they would one day come back for her. Annie wore the locket every day and every night throughout her hard-knock-life, Great Depression years in the downtown Manhattan orphanage. She wished on the locket for her parents to come and save her from the evil ways of Miss Hannigan. And while her parents never showed up, Daddy Warbucks saved her. Spoiler alert and added bonus interpretation: she saved him right back.

When my parents gave me a little Elsa Peretti gold heart necklace, which came perfectly packaged in a Tiffany blue box, for my sixteenth birthday, I thought for sure that it would be my one special, forever piece of jewelry. I convinced myself that I could wish on the purposely misshapen heart pendant and it would bring me good things, good luck, and generally a good life. I now recognize this mentality for what it truly was—magical thinking and quite possibly the beginnings of high-functioning, self-soothing, obsessive-compulsive behavior. I promised myself that I would never take off the magical necklace, and I didn't. I wore it every day and every night. I slept in it. I showered in it. I wore it in the summer with my super-classy white V-neck men's undershirts and in the winter dangling out of the folded-over neck part of my turtlenecks.

I wished on it the most unoriginal teenage wish imaginable. I wanted a boyfriend, a real-life serious boyfriend who would take me out on real-life dates, tell me he loved me, and treat me like I was his favorite person in the world. I knew I wouldn't find this boyfriend in high school. It was hard enough for me to fit in with the preppy, popular high school girls—hanging with the boys, and furthermore finding an actual human boy to be my boyfriend, was not even remotely on my horizon. When I had to ask a boy to my senior prom, I asked a junior.

I continued to wish for this boyfriend in college, where I hoped, prayed, and even legitimately suspected that the social scene would be more kind to me. It was. I met two more of my awesome, lifelong friends during the first semester of my freshman year. I know that I have, or at least claim to have, a lot of these awesome, lifelong friends. I've been lucky in the friendship department. Strong female friendships have always been important to me. Maybe it's because I never had any sisters. Or maybe it's because I went to an all-girls camp. Or maybe it's just that I love being with my friends. Like anything worth having, friendships are work, and I work hard at them. I am awesome at keeping in touch. Just ask my friends. My mom used to say that I collected friends and never let them go. I think there are a lot worse things than friends to collect—things like the tiny Royal Doulton miniature jugs that Neil collects and that freak me out when I walk by them late at night upstairs on our bookshelves because I think the miniature Henry VIII is giving me a creepy look.

Jill and Tracy were my first awesome, lifelong college friends. They lived in the loser freshman dorm with me, but they were really cool, genuine, and funny, and we did almost everything together, starting on the first night we met, as we crossed paths walking back to our loser dorm after freshman convocation. We studied together sometimes in the beautiful and quiet fine-arts library and sometimes in the ugly but much louder and more social main campus library, where we scoped out cute boys, wondering if they had girlfriends or not. We listened to Bruce Springsteen and the Indigo Girls in our dorm rooms, and we went to fraternity parties and to sketchy West Philadelphia bars with our even sketchier fake IDs.

Jill, Tracy, and I took what would become our first of many travel adventures together during the winter of our freshman year. We trained it down to Washington, DC, on the eve of President Clinton's first inauguration in January 1993. We patted ourselves on our backs for skipping class to bear witness to history. We slept side by side like three little monkeys in a bed. It was actually a basement futon in suburban DC that belonged to a boy we knew from our loser freshman dorm. He was a super-nice guy, although I don't think we talked to him much after that night. I still feel bad about that.

As our forty-second president gave his inaugural address, Jill, Tracy, and I roamed around the freezing cold National Mall, smiling at just about every young person who we suspected was skipping class, just like we were. My magical Elsa Peretti heart hung out over my white turtleneck and my navy-blue Penn sweatshirt.

We ran into a group of Georgetown and Penn students, some of whom Tracy knew from her hometown. One of the Penn students was an upperclassman, a boy named Danny. I had never met him or even seen him around Penn's campus. He would become my boyfriend, or, as my parents would call him, *the* boyfriend.

Danny ended up taking the train back with us to Philadelphia, in what I thought was another random run-in, this time at Union Station, but later learned was an engineered move for him to spend more time with me. He thought I was cute and funny, and as I talked to him for the two-and-a-half-hour train ride back to Thirtieth Street Station, and then on the cab ride back to campus, I began to see those same qualities in him. Within a few days, it was unofficially official: Danny was my boyfriend. I was his girlfriend. The magical heart pendant necklace had worked.

Danny was a great boyfriend. He took me out on dates to really nice restaurants in downtown Philadelphia and also to the crappy pizza and cheesesteak places on campus. He surprised me with little gifts. He wrote original poetry for me, and he helped me write my papers for classes that he had already taken the year before. We did all the college boyfriend-girlfriend stuff. We studied together. We went to parties together. We stayed up late into the night, talking about any and every ridiculous, absurd, or deep thought that came to mind. We slept over in each other's dorm rooms, sharing just a twin bed. Danny invited me to all the holidays at his parents' house, and I went. He wanted my parents to meet his parents. They did. I think that freaked my parents out. It kind of freaked me out, too, even though I really liked his parents.

Two years into our official boyfriend-girlfriend-ness, I left Penn to study abroad in London for my junior spring semester. Jill and Tracy came with me, and so did my awesome childhood friend Stacey. I was super excited for our European adventure. I imagined us visiting old British castles, wandering through the gardens of Kensington Palace while stalking Princess Diana, drinking tea and eating biscuits at fancy London hotels, and becoming regulars at casual neighborhood pubs.

I was sad and also a little nervous to leave Danny behind. He promised to write to me in London and to call and even email me, which was a big-deal, crazy thing to do in 1995. We talked about his coming to visit me. He mentioned something about meeting up in Paris for a romantic getaway. That sounded like a very real boyfriend-girlfriend thing to do.

Danny and I spent a lot of the winter break together before I left for London. We met up in New York City, where he bought me this funky silver ring with a green stone in it at Barneys. I thought it was really cool. It freaked my parents out.

"You kids are way too serious," my mother told me when she saw the ring. I think she thought we were getting engaged or something. I cried when winter break ended and I had to say goodbye to Danny, before he trained it back to college and I flew off to London. I wore the ring every day, and, of course, the Elsa heart as well. I wished on the heart that we would stay together. I had this feeling that we wouldn't.

London was awesome. Jill, Tracy, Stacey (I know, it rhymes), and I lived together in a fourth-floor flat above a Benetton store, across the street from a market that carried the most amazing hummus I have ever tasted. The flat came with a television that broadcast three channels—four if you counted the channel that connected to a camera over the building's main door. Sometimes we watched that channel. We had zero royal sightings, but we did tour several old British castles, and at night we went to pubs where we drank disgusting British beer. We loved going to afternoon tea, and we lingered way too long in the fancy British hotel lobbies, asking for second and then third servings of scones and biscuits.

I traveled with the girls all throughout Europe during long weekends and on extended breaks from British university. We visited my brother, Jonny, who was studying and living in a dorm room inside an old castle in Edinburgh. I had a crush on one of Jonny's British friends in Scotland, and I suspected he liked me, too, but I remained faithful to Danny, who I thought/hoped was pining away for me back at home. We visited friends in Spain and France and shared bunk beds with Australian and German strangers in Italian and Swiss hostels. On one excursion, Tracy and I slept in a weird old lady's spare bedroom in Prague, wondering if she was going to kidnap us and make us become her servants and citizens of the Czech Republic. She let us go just in time to make our train to Budapest.

Danny wrote fewer letters as the semester went on. He didn't call me as much, and we had some technical difficulties with the 1995 email system. My British university email address was made up of a slew of consonants that spelled nothing, the percentage sign, and four hyphens. Danny never came to visit. He told me that he was overwhelmed with graduate school applications and senior-year stuff. Jill's boyfriend found time to visit her. I wished harder and harder on the heart necklace. I didn't want to lose my real-life boyfriend.

I made excuses to Jill and Tracy and most of all to myself about Danny's quite obvious absence. I began to doubt him, to doubt the whole boyfriend-girlfriend thing, and to wonder what was wrong with me. I had been a good girlfriend. I was a good person. I never took off the heart necklace.

I broke down one afternoon during our travels in Florence. Right in front of Michelangelo's *David*, a full-blown, ugly, hiccupping cry came out of me. I had been keeping that cry locked deep inside me since we'd visited the Caso Battló in Barcelona nearly two weeks earlier. Jill and Tracy pulled me out of the way of the most famous penis statue in the world as they found a bench where we could all sit down in a corner of the Galleria.

"I think Danny may be breaking up with me," I said through a ton of snot and tears. I thought I saw Billy Crystal walk by us out of the corner of my eye. It wasn't him—just a short, middle-aged man with a close-shaven beard wondering why some American tourist girl was losing her shit near the *David*.

"It's okay, Rach," said Jill, drawing on her best notes from her psychology classes. After college, Jill got her PhD in psychology and became an awesome and renowned therapist. I've never paid her for her services, but I probably should have, or at least she should have taken money from my insurance company. She's the best listener, and whenever I get off the phone with her, I feel like I've just experienced at least three Oprah "aha" moments.

"You are going to be absolutely fine. You are the best, and you don't need Danny or any other boy to make you feel that way," Jill said. Tracy jumped in, telling me how even more awesome I was. (This is why I love my friends so much.) She told me how great senior year back at school would be without Danny. I could go out with just the girls, with other boys, with whomever I wanted to, or just be happy by myself. It was our own version of an "a woman needs a man like a fish needs a bicycle" talk.

When I returned home from my semester abroad that summer, Danny came to visit me at my parents' house. He slept with me in my twin bed in my childhood bedroom, woke up the next morning, and then broke up with me. I cried. I felt pathetic and, I am sure, looked even more pathetic as I hugged him goodbye, clinging to the last traces of the real-life boyfriend I'd thought I would have for the rest of my days.

That was the beginning of a really shitty summer. I worked at Bloomberg News, which sounds kind of cool now, but all I did that summer was enter data I couldn't understand into the space-like Bloomberg computer terminal while eating all the free snacks in the office, wondering why Danny had broken up with me. My pathetic sadness turned to anger as I learned that he had been cheating on me with some other girl back at school while I'd remained loyal to him the whole time I'd been in Europe.

My mother tried to cheer me up by taking me shopping. I agreed to go along with her, mainly because none of my clothes fit. All the British beer, British scones, and British biscuits had made their way directly to my ass.

"Boy, he really did a number on you," my mom said to me one hot Saturday in July as I moped around the Banana Republic in Princeton. "Come on, Rach, buck up. You have your whole life in front of you, and you'd better not miss out on it over this one boy. Daddy and I never liked him anyway," she said. They really didn't. She went on to tell me how some friend of hers I had never heard of had a son or a nephew or something who thought I was really cute and wanted to "take me out." I smiled briefly and tried on more black Banana Republic pants made for college girls with big asses.

My mother was right. Getting dumped by Danny was probably one of the best things that could have happened to me. "He did me a favor" was the line I would tell my friends back at college as we sat at the bar around the corner from our crappy off-campus house, drinking even crappier drinks.

My mother wondered why I still wore the Barneys ring that Danny had given me. She had a point. It was still a cool-looking ring, but it was very uncool to wear the ring given to you by a guy who cheated on you and then dumped you. I threw it out—in the trash. I thought about melting it down and molding the hot liquid silver into something else, but then I realized I was not a welder and that that would be even more pathetic than continuing to wear the ring in its original form.

I still wore the Elsa Peretti heart necklace. It was still my favorite everyday piece of jewelry. I still had my parents and my brother. They still loved me. I still had awesome friends. I still had a good life.

I went back to college for my senior year in my new big-assed-girl black pants and my long sweaters to cover up my big girl ass. I went out with other boys. I didn't wish for a boyfriend. I didn't really wish for anything. I just wore the necklace. I still thought it was really pretty and special, but I considered taking it off. And eventually I did.

Kate Spade and

Mary Tyler Moore

Most of my early knowledge and imagery of a young, working, single gal in the city came from reruns of *The Mary Tyler Moore Show*. Later on, it was from *Murphy Brown* and *Ally McBeal*, but really, Mary Richards was the gold standard. I wanted to be Mary. I wanted to live on my own in the big city and have an interesting and important job. I wanted to laugh with my quirky work family during the day and with my '90s versions of Rhoda Morgensterns at night. I wanted my own work desk, my own work phone, and, most important, my own workbag. I envisioned this workbag as somewhat like my father's leather briefcase, which I carried when I dressed up as a "businesswoman" for career day in fourth grade. My real workbag would be softer, more feminine, and probably not leather.

I channeled Mary the summer after I graduated from college, when I moved to New York City. I lived with three other girls in an Upper West Side two-bedroom—converted by two pop-up, paper-thin walls into four bedrooms—apartment. I got my Mary Richards television-station dream job, working in marketing at Time Inc. in the Time-Life Building, right across the street from Radio City Music Hall.

That was my second job. My first job was not so great. I kind of hated it. At the first job, I sold tiny, back-of-the-book ad space for computer magazines. I spent my days in a cubicle, calling start-up software and memory-storage companies, which I imagined were based out of graduate school students' Northern California apartments or mad scientists' basements. I left messages on answering machines, noting the times of my scripted messages in a very basic, mid-'90s sales software program. The only people who called me back were soon-to-be-out-of-money software designers and a few lonely wrong numbers.

I rarely left my cubicle because I didn't want any of my coworkers to see the horrid acne that had popped up all along my chin line and in my upper-lip area. I looked like I had a goatee made of painful, giant pimples. The irony was that I had beautiful, clear skin all throughout high school and college, when you're supposed to break out. The big zits showed up just as I was beginning a new life as a working gal. I didn't remember Mary's having had acne.

I went to see my grandmother's Upper East Side dermatologist, an older man with a full, dark beard, which I found really sketchy. I think a doctor who specializes in making his patients' faces look clear and beautiful should not cover up his own face. It's like going to a dentist with bad teeth or exercising with a fat trainer. The bearded dermatologist put me back on the pill, which cleared up my hormonal acne, which apparently is a thing.

"You just need the first job to get the second job, and that job will be so much better," my mother said to me when I called her from my cubicle to whisper to her about how painfully boring my work was.

"How's your face?" she asked, trying to change the subject.

"Not good. Not good at all," I whispered back to her.

"Just wear bright red lipstick," she replied. "Then people won't notice the pimples."

The lipstick didn't help. I did manage to figure out a secret path to the bathroom whereby I didn't have to walk by the cubicles of people I knew. Only a few strangers saw me whiz past as I covered up as much of my face as possible with my hair, leaving only a little space around my eyes so that I could see where I was going.

The second job came about a year into the first, and, as my mother predicted, it was better, way better. It helped that my skin had completely cleared up by then. I felt good about myself walking to work every day without having to worry about concealing my face with my hair. I wore sneakers for my twenty-block commute (very Melanie Griffith in *Working Girl*) and carried my work shoes in a workbag I had fashioned out of an old, woven book bag from college. Once inside the Time-Life Building, I grabbed my pass out from the old, woven bag and flashed it to the security guard who stood in front of my elevator bank. I felt special for having that badge, but really for having that job.

I worked on a team with mostly really smart, really interesting, and really fun people. One of those people was my college friend Henry. Henry was the one who told me about the job opening. He put in a good word for me with his boss's boss, who ran our team, and he even helped me rewrite my résumé and prep for the interview. My father still thanks Henry every time he sees him.

I worked on direct-marketing campaigns for some of my most favorite magazines: *Life*, *People*, and *InStyle*. I also got to work on marketing strategies for the launch of several then-new magazines, including *Real Simple*, *Teen People*, and *People en Español*, even though I couldn't speak or read a word of Spanish, having taken French in high school and college. I worked my ass off in a very real, hands-on, this-stuff-counts way that I never had in all my years of school. It wasn't brain surgery or rocket science, but sometimes it felt like it might have been. During my HR training session, my first week on the job, my hiring manager told me I was representing iconic publishing brands to the rest of the world. I heard that.

My team and I worked on tight deadlines and managed the design, implementation, and analysis of millions of pieces of promotions sent out all over the country. I flew down to our fulfillment house in Florida to check out the massive operations and see our strategies implemented up close and personal.

I was never bored at Time Inc.—not even in the slightest. I ran from meetings with executives in conference rooms, with artists at their drafting tables, with research experts who moderated focus groups with the magazine's readers, back to my office, where I had two desks—one for my computer and one for all my important papers. My parents were most impressed with the fact that I had my own office and that a car service took me to and from the airport for business trips. My mom also liked how, when she called me at work, I was always "unavailable," or at least that's what it said on my voice mail, where she left her cryptic messages.

"Hello, this is Rebecca Levy, calling in regard to a business matter. Please call me back when you have a chance. You have the number. Thank you." And then she hung up. I called her back and explained that I was the only person who ever listened to my voice messages.

The only downside of my big-girl Mary Richards dream job was that my boss was kind of a nightmare. Her name was Lucy, and my HR hiring manager told me she was a "marketing genius." Lucy had an Ivy League pedigree and an MBA from a top-ten business school. She had a solid reputation from another prestigious publishing company and came highly recommended to Time Inc. by some big-shot muckety-mucks. She had just started working at Time when I was hired. I thought she was weird when she interviewed me—she had this crazy-eyes look about her—but I didn't care that much. I wanted the job.

As I got to know Lucy, I figured out that she was indeed weird. On Monday mornings, during our obligatory "How was your weekend?" chats in her office across the hall from mine, she told me about how she and her husband took turns reading a book to each other—out loud. She had no idea how to use Excel or PowerPoint, and she typed like a seven-year-old. Her spelling was abysmal, and I thought she had ADD—that or a natural-born twitch. Otherwise, she was great. Lucy flew down the hallway with frenetic speed from meeting to meeting as she yelled for me to walk with her, then whispered loudly that she would explain everything on the way. I asked Henry what he thought of her behavior. He advised me to keep my head down and do my work. And so I did. I did everything Lucy asked me to do, and then, by necessity, I did more. I corrected her work when she wasn't looking and eventually when she asked me to look it over for her.

Lucy stayed at work later than anyone in my group, and she came in on the weekends. I'm not really sure what she did with all that extra time in the office, because her work still had a gazillion mistakes. I continued to correct them. Her eyes started to look super-crazy-ish, and the twitch became more noticeable. I wondered if Lucy's boss, Janie, noticed. She did.

"Why don't you take a long lunch?" Janie said to me one morning, as she popped her head into my office.

I looked at my watch. It was 10:00 a.m. "Sure," I said, and then put down Lucy's latest report, which I was editing for her. I called college friend Penny, who worked at an advertising agency a few blocks away, and asked if she could meet me outside in Rockefeller Center for an early lunch. She could meet me, but not right away. I walked in circles around Rock Center about thirty times, wondering what the hell was going on inside the Time-Life Building, as I watched the tourists leaving the area around the *Today* show studio.

Penny and I chatted over our giant, make-your-own salads from our favorite deli as we thought of the craziest scenarios playing out back at my office. Penny hugged me and told me to relax. She was sure I would be okay. I thought I would be but also wondered if Lucy might take me down with her.

When I got back to the office, Janie informed me that Lucy had been fired. She had been escorted out of the building by security just as I was eating my giant salad with Penny. I wasn't alone in my Lucy suspicions. It turned out that Lucy had no freaking idea what she was doing. She had screwed up some major big-deal things for some major big-deal people. Janie was so nice to me. She sat in my office for what felt like forever and told me that my job was more than secure. I would get a new, great boss who would actually teach me things. In the meantime, though, I should go to Janie for anything—anything at all. I thanked Janie and told her I understood. I wanted to ask her how Lucy had even been hired in the first place and who had recommended her, but I didn't. I heard Henry's voice in my mind: *Keep your head down.* I realized that you could be a complete moron, even if you went to an Ivy League college and got your MBA from a top-ten school.

My second boss, Amy, was hired just a few weeks later. Amy was an internal hire and had a solid reputation within the company. She seemed great to me. She was super nice to me and super fun, too. She took me out to lunch all the time and stopped by my office to chitchat about actual normal stuff, like running in the park, which she did in lieu of reading a book out loud to her grown-man husband, on the weekends. Amy was the anti-Lucy. She didn't have the highbrow-weirdo-intellectual vibe that Lucy did. She struck me more as a popular college party girl. She seemed to have street smarts and good instincts, and she was a people person. I thought she would be great in sales. She praised my work and gave me only positive feedback. I could see us working together for a long time. I sensed Amy wouldn't teach me a whole lot, but I wouldn't have to correct her mistakes, and she was not a lunatic.

About six months into Amy's tenure as my boss, Janie came into my office late one afternoon and closed my door behind her. I was a little nervous.

"Rach," she said. Even though Janie was my senior by two levels, we were still on a one-syllable-name basis. I liked Janie a lot, and I knew she was really the brains behind our operation. She managed our whole team, and she made it look easy. She was fun and smart and approachable, but she also held me, and everyone on her team, to a high standard.

"We had to fire Amy," Janie told me.

I was stunned. I couldn't react in a way that would have made any sense to me or to Janie. Security had escorted Amy out of the building earlier in the afternoon. She had been stealing and selling items from the company storage closet— the one that contained magazine-branded paraphernalia like *Sports Illustrated* sweatshirts and *People* tote bags.

"Hmm," I managed to say to Janie. "I did not see that coming."

Janie smiled, then laughed. We both laughed. She took me out for drinks that night after work. We talked about a lot of work stuff and also about a lot of nonwork stuff. She didn't reassure me like she had when security escorted my first boss out of the building. She didn't have to. I knew Janie would take care of me. I also knew that I didn't need as much taking care of as I had back when I'd started working there, almost a year and a half earlier. I had kept my head down and learned how to do my job, and, in the process, how to do both Lucy's and, by default, Amy's.

I reported directly to Janie as she searched for a new, noncrazy version of Lucy and a new, nonkleptomaniac one of Amy. The search took longer than either Janie or I had expected. At some point, I stopped paying attention to the search process. I was busy and a little bit obsessed with working on the *Real Simple* launch. Janie let me in on all aspects of the new magazine. I was one of just a few people who knew about the concept, and we spoke softly and in code about the not-yet-named publication. It felt very government spy–like, in a women's-magazine-launch kind of way.

At the end of one of our closed-door launch meetings, Janie stayed behind in the conference room until it was just the two of us sitting there. She told me that they were offering my new boss's job to me. I was shocked. Janie and the higher-ups realized that I had been doing my job and my boss's job for pretty much the whole time I had been there, and that they would be crazy not to give me the boss's job. That's what Janie said. I swear.

I moved into a bigger office. I moved into a higher pay grade. I had more responsibility and more work. I managed other people. I decided that I would be the best boss. I would be fun and caring, and I would teach my reports anything and everything they ever wanted to know. I wouldn't go crazy, and I wouldn't steal from the company store.

I called my parents that night from my office at work to

tell them the big news. They were away in Europe. I waited until it was late enough that night that it wouldn't be too early for them the next morning at their hotel. I woke them up. My mother answered the phone with her *I hope you're not dead* voice.

"Mom," I said, "I got a promotion. They gave the boss's job to me. I'm the boss now."

"Jimmy, wake up," I heard her say, as she presumably shook my father in the bed next to her. "They made Rach the boss. She's a big shot."

They each got on the phone with me and separately gushed about how proud of me they were. I thanked them. I told them I loved them. They loved me, too. I hung up. I looked down at my old, woven makeshift workbag below my desk. It looked rattier than ever. I threw my work papers and my work shoes in it as I changed into my sneakers, planning my walk home to the Upper West Side.

I made a last-minute decision to walk east, instead of west, as I left the Time-Life Building that night. I went to Bloomingdale's. College friend Lauren worked as a buyer at Bloomingdale's and was the most fashion-forward friend/ person I knew. She carried an oversize, boxy black nylon Kate Spade bag to work with her every day. I admired her bag many times but told myself it was too big a purchase for me to make. But then I realized that, compared with the bags Carrie Bradshaw had on *Sex and the City*, the Kate Spade bag was mere chump change. Carrie would have used the Kate Spade bag as a toilet case.

I walked into Bloomingdale's that night, past the per-fume-spritzing ladies, with clarity and purpose and headed right over to the Kate Spade bags. I selected the oversize, boxy black nylon one, just like Lauren's. I glanced at myself in the full-length mirror, thinking how perfect the bag looked hanging down over my pantsuit jacket. It felt even better.

"I'll take it," I said to the saleslady, flashing as big a Mary Richards smile as I could. I paid for it, asked her to remove the tags, and then filled the bag with my stuff from the tattered, woven college bag.

I walked out onto Lexington Avenue that night with my new big-girl workbag, my even bigger big-girl smile, and a Mary Richards swing in my step. Had I been wearing a hat, I would have thrown it up in the air. I had made it after all.

Chan Luu and

Growing Together

I met my husband at a party I almost didn't go to. My original plan for the night of the party was to hang out in my two-bedroom-cum-four-bedroom apartment with my roommates and watch movies I'd already seen a thousand times on TBS. But then college friend Kara called, insisting that I meet her and her boyfriend, Steve, out at this party Steve's friend was hosting at a neighborhood bar.

I was hesitant when I clicked over to my call-waiting call and heard my mother's cheery checking-in voice. I told her of my impending evening plans. She wondered why I wouldn't go out with Kara. My mother always loved a good party. I clicked back to Kara and agreed to meet her at the party—"for just one drink," I told her.

Kara and Steve were already at the party when I arrived, and I knew a lot of other people there. Steve was also a good friend of mine from college, and throughout our college years I had met many of his friends whom he had known since childhood—except for one. His name was Neil. When I showed up, Neil was chatting away and joking with Steve. He shook my hand firmly, looking me right in the eye, as Steve introduced us, cracking a joke about Neil's new George Clooney–esque haircut. I trusted a firm handshake as much as I mistrusted a weak one, and I liked the haircut.

Neil and I talked almost exclusively to each other that night, about the basic résumé stuff—where we had grown up, where we had gone to school, and what we did for work. We also talked about some of the not-so-basic résumé stuff as I shared with him what I thought to be witty stories of family and friends. He outwitted me with his own anecdotes and observations about his new haircut and the weird, flowy black pants I was wearing that night. I think the pants confused him. He was more of a jeans guy. Clearly, he knew nothing about mid-'90s fashion, but he was really funny. He had a nice smile, and his eyes looked warmer when he smiled.

After a few hours of free-flowing conversation and free-flowing cheap drinks, I was ready to head home to my apartment, to my roommates, and maybe to some late-night movies on TBS. Steve insisted on walking Kara and me home. Before I could grab my bag, Neil was by my side. He wanted to walk us home, too.

The four of us ended up going out for dessert en route to my apartment. Neil ordered cannoli, and we split them. He was impressed that I knew the line about the cannoli and the guns from *The Godfather*. I was impressed that he shared the cannoli with me even though I told him that I didn't want any dessert.

Neil, Kara, and Steve left me off in front of my building. I gave each one of them a kiss on the cheek, saving Neil for last, unsure whether my gesture was appropriate. As I pulled away from him, he asked if I wanted to go out with him sometime. I giggled at his formality. I agreed.

When I showed up five minutes late for our first official date less than a week later, I caught a glimpse of Neil waiting patiently for me at the end of a long bar at a new Upper West Side open-concept-kitchen restaurant. I would later learn that he was always five minutes early. I got a pit, the good kind, if that's possible, in my stomach as I watched him watching for me. He seemed different than other boys I had dated. And he was a boy at just twenty-three years old, just as I was a girl at twenty-two. He seemed like a real, genuine person, salt of the earth, which was what a future mutual friend of ours would later call him. He didn't strike me as the type who played games or put on airs—and definitely not as the kind who would cheat on me or break my heart. I thought this could turn into something.

We split a bottle of wine at the open-concept-kitchen restaurant. I talked a lot at the beginning of dinner. He talked more as the night went on. His dry sense of humor caught me off guard. My giggles turned into fits of laughter. When I got up to go to the bathroom, I realized I was a little drunk. He kissed me in the narrow fifth-floor hallway just outside my apartment door after dinner. I knew I would go out with him again. And I did—again and again and again.

We hung out with Neil's hilarious friends and room-mates in his two-bedroom-cum-three-bedroom apartment down in the Meatpacking District back when they actually packed meat in that neighborhood, long before Tory Burch and rag & bone had storefronts there. I slept over at his place when we went out downtown on the weekends, staying warm in his full-size bed, underneath his Mexican blanket, which he kept as room decor from a college spring-break trip to Cancun. I made chocolate-chip pancakes for Neil and his roommates one Sunday morning in the most disgusting galley kitchen I had ever seen. It still smelled like buffalo wings from the last time the boys had cooked in there—several months before then, for a big football game on television. They declared it the best day their kitchen ever saw. I took that as the highest compliment.

Neil came over to my apartment most weeknights. We made spaghetti together, or breaded chicken, which he named Chicken Rach. I often burned the chicken and occasionally set off the smoke alarm, but we still ate it. We watched movies we had seen before and tried to impress each other with the lines we knew. He slept over in my full-size bed—the one with the flowered Ralph Lauren quilt I had bought at Bloomingdale's. We went out to movies at the Lincoln Square Theater near my apartment or to the Angelika near his. We went to parties hosted by his friends or my friends or friends of those friends. We were usually the first people to leave the parties and go home with each other. I was always more than ready and happy to go home with him.

Neil had an idea that we should each put away twenty bucks in a pot at the end of every week. We would do this until we had saved up enough money to go to one of the fancy NYC restaurants he wanted to try. I didn't really care that much about the fancy city restaurant scene, or food in general, for that matter, but I agreed to his plan. We went to One If by Land, Two If by Sea, Gramercy Tavern, Union Square Cafe, and others. I figured out that putting the money in the pot for future dates was Neil's own way of securing future dates with me. He wanted to see me more. He was serious about me. I was serious about him.

Neil bought me the requisite serious-boyfriend gifts. For my birthday, he gave me pearl earrings from Fortunoff, and for our one-year dating anniversary—yes, we were that couple that celebrates dating anniversaries—he bought me Tiffany silver bean earrings and a matching silver bean bracelet. I wore the bean bracelet to work and shook it around during meetings to make sure my coworkers noticed my serious-boyfriend bracelet.

I moved out of my two-bedroom-cum-four-bedroom apartment into a tiny one-bedroom apartment. It was more like a studio with a wall thrown in a rather arbitrary place, resulting in a long, skinny, aisle-like bedroom and a microscopic, triangular living space. I managed to fit my Jennifer Convertibles pullout couch and my Pottery Barn wicker chair into the living space. The chair backed up to the giant heating pipe, which could burn your skin if you happened to touch it during one of its middle-of-the-night steam fits.

Neil proposed to me in the tiny apartment, next to the giant heating pipe. He surprised me one night after work by greeting me on one knee, with an engagement ring in hand, as I walked in the door. He was supposed to be traveling for business that night. My doorman, Richard, whose Starbucks order we knew, had let Neil in and even helped him set up the proposal staging in my apartment.

I screamed and then cried as he put the ring on my finger. Neil had notified my friends and his of the impending engagement. They came over within a few minutes of my saying yes. We celebrated that night with champagne, tortilla chips, and pretzels, squeezing onto the Jennifer Convertibles couch and the Pottery Barn chair. Some friends sat on my bed. I called my parents with the good news. They had known it was coming, as Neil had already called them, quite formally, to ask for my hand in marriage. They were excited for us. They didn't say anything about being worried that we were too young to get married at just twenty-five and twenty-six, but I later learned they were.

Neil proposed with an emerald-cut engagement ring set in platinum. He had paid for it with his bar mitzvah money. He knew I wanted the same ring that my mom had because I had flat out told him. He also knew where to get it, as Penny had hooked him up with her sister-in-law Debbie, who worked in the diamond business. I later asked Debbie about their secret meetings in midtown, inspecting cut-up precious rocks together while Neil did his very best to make sure he bought me just what I wanted. He did, but I feel bad and also embarrassed now about the engagement ring–zilla that I let myself become. I was stupid. I was young. Neil was young, too.

Our wedding was only the second wedding Neil had attended. The first was that of Kara and Steve, who eventually took full credit for our meeting, our marriage, and our kids' existences, having "set us up" at that party that I almost didn't go to. Our wedding felt more like my mother's wedding. She planned every last detail with the help of her older sister, my aunt Jo, who has amazing taste in everything. I had input on the cake, selecting one that was made of cupcakes. Neil had input on our registry, selecting beer steins. That was pretty much it for us, and we were completely fine with that.

Neil gave me another requisite gift the week before our wedding—a small silver chain-link bracelet with tiny diamonds in it. I gave him a fancy watch. I wore the bracelet to our wedding, and he wore the watch. I'm not sure we ever wore them again. They seemed way too formal, way too not us.

Early married life was not that different from our dating life. Neil had moved into my tiny one-bedroom, one-giant-heating-pipe apartment right after we got engaged. He showed up on moving day with his Mexican blanket and his small bedroom television. Everything else he owned that was worth keeping was already at my apartment, as he had slept there every night for a long time. We didn't add his name to our answering machine or to the mailbox until after we got married, having wanted to avoid needing to explain to my grandparents that we were living in sin.

We cooked more crappy dinners together and ordered in only slightly better Chinese, Indian, and Thai dinners. We hung out with both of our sets of friends, who had become legitimate friends with each other. Some even dated.

We left New York City two years into our marriage to attend graduate school together in Michigan. We knew no one in Ann Arbor. We made new friends. We studied together. We cooked together. We went out to bars and parties together. Our new business school friends couldn't quite wrap their heads around the fact that we were a married couple and that both of us were students together. "It's like college," I explained to my fellow Wolverines, "only we always have a date."

Ann Arbor was a chance for us to get away from a place where we had once existed as separate people. Everyone in Ann Arbor knew us as Rachel and Neil, the married students. "It's your Little Rock," my aunt Jo told me, comparing our two years in business school to the time she had spent, a generation earlier, away with her then-new young husband, my uncle Dick, in Little Rock, Arkansas, while Uncle Dick was stationed in the Air Force. *Kind of? Maybe?* I liked that analogy.

We gave up on the requisite gift giving in Ann Arbor, shopping on a much more limited graduate school student budget. Neil bought me a yoga mat for my birthday. I went to a few classes at the gym on campus, using my student ID to get a discount. I bought him a case of his favorite Michigan beer, Bell's Oberon. He had his new business school friends over to drink it with him. They were hilarious, too.

We graduated from business school. We moved to suburban Philadelphia, near where I grew up. Neil got a job offer at the Philadelphia office of the management consulting firm he had worked at before business school, but in New York. I got a job at a small marketing and branding firm in the suburb we soon called home. I got pregnant. We had a baby boy and, a couple years later, a baby girl. We took care of the babies. Neil took care of me. I took care of him.

We left our babies at home one night with the nanny we had hired to take care of them while we both worked during the day. She was our third nanny in a slew of eight. Or maybe it was nine? I can't remember. We went out to celebrate our real anniversary—not a dating one. I also can't remember what number it was, but I do remember being happy to be out with Neil on a real, no-kids date night.

He handed me a velvet pouch, no wrapping paper. In it was a pair of dangly earrings. They had tiny gold circles hanging down a delicate gold-link chain, and the post of each earring was one long, skinny piece of gold meant to hang down as well. They were so funky, so cool. I adored them. Neil had picked them out all by himself at this tiny, trendy boutique that he knew I loved in town. He had never heard of the designer, Chan Luu, but I had. I had admired her wrap bracelets and dangly earrings on other people. Neil just thought they "looked like me," or so he told me that night.

They did look like me, and they felt like me, too—way more me than the Tiffany bean bracelet, which was tarnished and which I never wore anymore. The pearl earrings Neil had long ago given me had not seen the light of day in years, and I was pretty sure I had lost the wedding-present bracelet. I still wear my emerald-cut engagement ring every day. I love it, but not because it was what I thought I should have or what my mother had. I love it because Neil spent the time and effort to find it with Penny and Debbie. I love, but still feel a little bit bad, that he spent his bar mitzvah money on it. He was so proud to have picked out that ring for me. And I could see on his face on the night of that anniversary dinner that he was so proud of having picked out the Chan Luu earrings for me, too.

In 2018, we have been together for over twenty years, married for nineteen. There are no more requisite gifts. He gets things for me that feel more me than ever—things like cozy long sweaters and scarves and funkier long earrings and even longer and funkier necklaces. I'm better at buying gifts for him, too. He tells me I pick out the best flannel shirts for him at J.Crew and the best North Face fleeces online at Zappos. "How did you know I would love it? That it would fit?" he asked me after the first night of Hanukkah in 2017. I just know now, and so does he.

When we first met, when we were kids, we fell in love. This is not a unique story. But then, somehow, and I think there was a fair bit of luck involved, we managed to grow up and grow together. I think I love Neil now more than I did when I married him.

I have seen people grow apart, people I love. I get how that happens. I'm amazed it doesn't happen more. How did I know that the guy with the dry sense of humor waiting for me at the end of the bar that night at the open-concept-kitchen Upper West Side restaurant would grow into the guy who makes my daughter and me laugh so hard that we get violent hiccups? How did I know he would spend endless hours talking ad nauseam to our son about the NFL and the NBA and that he would become the best middle-school social studies tutor? How did I know that he would understand and appreciate my own family in almost the same way I do? How did I know that he would make new friends whom I would really like and that he would like my new friends, too? How did I know that we would both want to live in an old house we'd be willing to renovate and send our kids to the school we do and teach them how to ski and play tennis? How did he know that I'd be totally okay with his sometimes-crazy work and travel schedules? How did he know that I would learn how to cook chicken without burning it or that I would learn how to play golf and that he would actually enjoy playing with me when his real golf friends were busy? He didn't know. I didn't know. *How could we have?*

I knew that he was a good guy, that he made me laugh, and that we had a good time together. I still tell him how funny he is, and he tells me I'm funny, too. I still tell him I think he's great. He tells me I look cute when I'm feeling so not cute in an oversize sweater and yoga pants. I rub his shoulders when he seems stressed, hunching over his computer in his J.Crew flannel shirt. I honestly think he's cuter now bald, having shaven off the Clooney hairdo a long time ago. He tells me I'm pretty even as my daughter counts the growing number of deep-set lines on my forehead. I tell him I'm way too scared to inject poison into my face, and so he'd better get used to the lines and maybe even to grays when I get sick of getting my hair colored every three weeks.

We are each other's biggest cheerleaders, having figured out long ago that the world is full of enough people who don't live in our house who can make us feel like shit. Of course, we give each other shit sometimes. I am not June Cleaver or Carol Brady. And he is definitely not Ward or Mr. Brady. The shit is also part of the deal. But we let the shit go or we laugh about it, or we forget about it before it ever gets too real.

I eventually lost one of the Chan Luu earrings. I wore them to a fund-raiser at our children's school, where I ended up trying on a few pairs of earrings for sale. When I got home that night and looked in the mirror, I realized that one of the Chan Luu earrings was missing. I searched myself, my car, my bag, and my clothes. I called the school the next day. I even went back to the parking lot. No dice.

I was bummed, bordering on sad, and becoming slightly obsessed. I told Neil about the missing earring. He didn't think much of it. "See if you can get a replacement one," he suggested. I never looked into it. I kept the single Chan Luu earring. I still have it. I'll never wear it as a single earring because I am not Cyndi Lauper, but I will also never get rid of it. I might look for a replacement one day, but I haven't gotten around to it.

I guess I figure I'm lucky enough to still have Neil—to still feel genuinely happy, even excited, to see him at the end of the day when I hear the garage door go up and his car pull in.

I understand and fully appreciate that we have grown together when we perhaps could have grown apart. That feels like enough.

Fleece Socks Will Keep You Warm at the University of Insomnia at Ann Arbor

I had never pulled an all-nighter—not even in college, when it felt like everyone else did. I couldn't stay up that late. My brain started to shut down around 11:00 p.m., which was about the time I'd leave the library and head back to my dorm room/off-campus house to get a good night's sleep. I was one of those annoying people whose eyes roll into the back of their skull in REM sleep pretty soon after their head hits the pillow. That all changed when I lived in Ann Arbor.

Neil had always intended to get his MBA, as most everyone at his firm had one. I applied to the same schools he did, in a last-minute Hail Mary move, and was pleasantly surprised/shocked when I was accepted to a few of them. I weighed the pros and cons of getting my MBA along with Neil and quickly figured out that the pros far outweighed the cons. We moved to Ann Arbor during the summerof 2001. We loved living in Ann Arbor. We loved going to school together. Well, I did. Neil said he felt like he was going to throw up every time I spoke in class, as he never knew what I was going to say. He was a little scared I was going to mess up in a big way answering a question posed by one of our world-renowned economics or finance professors. He had a point. I had no formal business education, having majored in history back in college. My pedigree screamed liberal arts, but somehow the University of Michigan thought I was worthy of earning an advanced business degree from it.

My parents called me one Monday night on our landline during our first fall in Ann Arbor. Neil answered in the living room, taking a break from watching a football game on TV. I was studying in the second bedroom–office of our garden apartment. Neil turned off the football game. He told me to pick up the phone in the office as he stayed on the line in the living room.

"Rach," my mom said in a shaky voice, "remember how I told you I had to get off the phone the other morning to head down to Philly?"

"Yes," I said, wondering why Neil was listening on another phone and why my mom sounded so weird. I realized that I had never asked her why she was rushing to downtown Philadelphia that day. I figured she was headed down for a lunch outing with her friends or maybe to the Philadelphia Museum of Art, which she loved.

"I was getting my PET scans then," she explained. My mother was diagnosed with ocular melanoma, a rare form of cancer, which starts out in the eye, in 1998. The tumor was discovered after she had severe blurriness in her right eye. The tumor was irradiated at Wills Eye Hospital in Philadelphia, and her prognosis was good. Her body scans were clear, and the protocol was to come back every six months for follow-up scans. Just weeks after she underwent the radiation, life seemed to go back to normal. I didn't think about it that much. I wasn't sure if she did.

"The scans showed tumors in my liver. The melanoma from my eye has spread," she explained, her voice still shaky but punctuated by a smile I could tell she was forcing onto her face for me and for her. I could hear my father's breath. He was on another phone in their house. "I'm seeing a wonderful doctor at Jefferson, right in Philadelphia, and they have a plan for me." I remember her saying something about experimental treatments, new medicines, and monthly visits to the hospital.

"Do you have any questions?" she asked, her voice rising with the hope that she hadn't just shattered my world.

"Nope," I said, as I felt my head pounding from trying to digest the information and holding in tears. I started to cry. She did, too. My father told me he loved me. My mother did, too. Neil put down the phone in the living room, came into the office, and stood behind me, rubbing my shoulders. I told them I loved them, too. They told me to get a good night's sleep and that we would talk again in the morning. I agreed to the plan and hung up.

I didn't know much about my mother's prognosis that night, but I kind of knew that life would never be the same.

I asked Neil questions he couldn't answer: What is this medicine? Will it work? Will she be okay? Will she die? How can she die? She's so young. She looks so healthy. How does a tumor go from an eye to a liver? I cried some more, and then I went to bed.

I couldn't fall asleep. I watched Neil with envy as he slept soundly next to me. I got up and walked into the living room. I grabbed a framed picture from our bookshelf. It was a great picture, from my cousin's wedding the previous summer—one of Neil and Jonny and my parents and me. My mom looked so tiny standing in between my six-foot-two-inch-tall father and six-foot-tall Neil. Her glasses rested on the top of her head so that the camera properly captured her giant, sparkly blue eyes. My eyes were blue but not as sparkly as hers and much smaller. I still didn't understand how that tumor, that fucking tumor, which I thought radiation had destroyed, had made its way into her liver.

I kissed her cute face through the glass picture frame. I kissed it twenty-three times—my lucky number and also the date of my birthday. I had never done that before. I had made wishes when the clock was at 11:11, said "rabbit, rabbit" when I woke up on the first of the month, and even stepped over a few cracks when I was younger. I felt a tiny bit relieved after the kissing. I went back to bed. I wished to whoever would listen to me that the medicine would work and that my mom would be okay. I said it twenty-three times. "Please let the medicine work and let my mom be okay." The last time I looked at the clock, it was after 3:00 a.m. I awoke the next morning at seven to get ready for class. I was tired. I was sad. I was scared.

My parents established a new normalcy back at home, driving down to Jefferson University Hospital in Philadelphia, along with my aunt Jo, every four weeks so that the cutting-edge oncologist could inject even more cutting-edge medications into my mother's liver. I called my mother every day. I sent her funny cards and emails. I started to hear a more genuine smile back in her voice. She was optimistic. She always was, and so was my father—maybe too optimistic? The doctors told them that the experimental medicine was working. The tumors were shrinking.

I was happy to hear this news, but I still couldn't sleep— at least not for more than a couple hours at a time. I wished more and more in my head and sometimes out loud in the shower or on a long walk in the gray and way-too-cold Ann Arbor fall air that the medicine would work and my mom would be okay. I said this so much, it became some kind of mantra. I kissed the picture of her face twenty-three times every night before I went to sleep. I didn't let Neil see me do this, but I imagine he wondered why I took so much time to come to bed. He knew that I was tired and sad and scared.

I pulled my first all-nighter in Ann Arbor. I didn't mean to. It was the night before my accounting final. I had studied really hard for it. Business school was good for my worried, scared, and sad brain. I threw myself into my studies, learning about capital financial models, accounting balance sheets, and economics theories of diminishing returns. I knew the material for the accounting final. I wasn't worried about that—I was worried about my mother. Even though the doctors told us that her tumors were shrinking and her scans looked good, I knew—buried somewhere way deep down inside me—that this wouldn't always be the case. I knew that even my young, strong, and beautiful mother couldn't survive metastatic tumors in her liver. I think my family knew it. I think my friends knew it. We didn't talk about it.

We followed my mother's lead. She went to the hospital very early in the morning once a month. She had experimental medicines injected into her. She got her blood drawn. She took her antibiotics to prevent infections. She had PET scans. She never complained. She relayed only the good news, at least to me. She lived her life. She traveled with my father. She went out with her friends. She shopped with her sister. She played golf—sometimes the day after a new treatment. She refused to give in to the tumors, to the fear, to the what-ifs.

I tried not to, either, but I found that to be more challenging. My brain was racked with the really bad what-ifs the night before my accounting final. I couldn't sleep. The wishing and the kissing of the picture didn't help. I looked at the clock at 2:00 a.m., 3:00 a.m., 4:00 a.m., and 5:00 a.m. When Neil's alarm clock went off at 7:00 a.m., I was sitting up in bed next to him, staring at the small, blank television screen in our bedroom. I told him I had been up literally all night. I'm not sure he believed me. I'm not sure I would have believed me if I hadn't actually done it.

I took the accounting final. I actually did okay on it. I came back to our apartment and fell asleep on our Jennifer Convertibles couch. When I woke up, Neil was sitting at the end of the couch. He lifted my feet up onto his lap. I cried a little bit. My head hurt. I was sad to see how sad he looked when he looked at me. We had a long talk. We agreed that I should "talk to someone." He was really worried about me. I was kind of worried about me but still more worried about my mom. I kept asking myself what would happen if the medicine stopped working, if my mom got really sick, if she died. I couldn't imagine a world without her in it.

I found a therapist on campus through the University of Michigan's health care system, which I highly recommend. If you are going to lose your shit, not sleep at night, and live day to day on the verge of a nervous breakdown, Ann Arbor is a great place to be. My therapist's name was Michelle. She was a short, middle-aged woman with a warm, round face and an even warmer smile. She had really short, spiky black hair, and she wore button-down shirts, khaki pants, and Timberland boots to all of our sessions.

In our very first session, I told her everything as I sat in an oversize chair catty-corner to the upright one that she sat in. I told her I had the best mother in the whole world, that we were very close, that she was only fifty-four, and that she had tumors in her liver. They had spread from her eye—her big, beautiful, sparkly blue eye. I didn't realize how angry I was until I talked to Michelle. I asked her why this had to happen to my mom. My mom was the best person. She never did anything wrong. That wasn't true, but anger, sadness, and disbelief will make you say things like that. There were so many crappy people walking around in the world with perfectly healthy livers. Why the fuck did my mother have to have tumors in hers?

Michelle didn't answer any of my questions. I guess I didn't expect her to. She asked me more questions, ones that I could answer. She asked me about my mom. I gushed.

I talked about how she had always been my biggest cheer-leader, how much fun we had together, how we shopped together and laughed together, how she had just sent me a framed sketch of two female stick figures with their arms around each other that said at the top, "One of the nicest things about being mother and daughter is that one day you discover you've turned into friends."

I noticed Michelle had a small gay-pride flag on her desk, which sat behind her chair. I wondered if she had a girlfriend. I imagined Michelle would be a really good girlfriend. She was a really good listener. I wondered if Michelle's mom was still alive. Were they close? Was she thinking about her when I told her about my mom?

Michelle prescribed me sleep aids. I took Ambien a couple times, but it didn't really help. Maybe I slept a bit more, but I felt hungover the next day. I was scared I would get hooked on the meds she gave me, even though my medical school friends told me I had the least addictive personality of anyone they had ever known. Even so, I took my remaining Ambien pills and flushed them down the toilet, like any good recovering drug addict.

I managed to make new friends in Ann Arbor, even in my depressed and anxious state. I must say, I hid it pretty well, saving the really batshit-crazy stuff for Neil, for phone calls with my college girls back in New York, and for my middle-of-the-night kissing fits with the picture of my mother.

My first business school friend was Shane. I had met her at the sell-the-program-to-new-students weekend the previous spring, and I had known then that if we both ended up in Ann Arbor, we would be friends. She was adorable. She was fun, oozed tons of energy, and had even less of a business background than I did. I was instantly attracted to her crazy head of giant light blond curls and her up-for-anything attitude. She was the first person, besides Neil and my finance professor—to whom I cried uncontrollably during his office hours—whom I told about my mom. Shane gave me a huge hug when I spilled the sad beans to her.

"It's okay, Rach," she said. "My dad died of cancer when I was in college. It's horrible, but you're going to be okay."

Died? Who said anything about dying? I pushed those what-if thoughts way down below, into my nervous gut, where they belonged. I listened to Shane's story, to her dad's story. I was sad for Shane, and then I was amazed at how happy she was, at what a good life she managed to be living. *That wouldn't be me*, I told myself. These medicines would work on my mom. She could take them forever, or at least until they invented the next medicine or the next treatment to cure Stage IV metastatic cancer.

I opened up to my other business school friend Tara, who became my unofficial tutor. Tara was an engineer and knew everything we needed to know for every single subject in business school. And if she didn't know it, she figured it out and taught it to me. *I should have become an engineer.* With Tara, I didn't bust out my "I think my mom may be dying, but I'm too sad to go there with you right now" story right away, the way I did with Shane, but eventually I got there.

One night, Shane and a couple of the other fun, cool, "I can see myself being friends with you in real life" business school girls planned a sleepover party for our group of five. We slept at Shane's apartment. We stayed up late, eating ice cream, drinking wine, and talking. I opened up a lot that night about my mom, about how I wasn't really dealing so well with the news and with life in general. They had no idea. I guess I didn't, either.

Tara came over to my garden apartment the next day with a cute card and an even cuter pair of gray fleece socks. "To keep you warm here in Michigan," the note said. I cried a little bit. And then I felt just a tiny bit better. It felt good to know that I could tell people about the tumors in my mother's liver, and the what-ifs in my head, and the sleep challenges, and could see that the world didn't fall apart as a result. My Ann Arbor friends didn't judge me for being a freak, for not sleeping, for flushing prescription sleep aids down the toilet in the middle of the night. They thought I was normal. They thought I was okay. They told me I would be okay no matter what. A little part of me started to believe them.

Neil was happy I had my own people in Ann Arbor. He had easily made friends with the giant crew of guys in business school. Note to all the single ladies out there: There are way more guys than girls in business school. If you want to find a cute, eligible, single guy, go get an MBA. Obviously, you should go to business school for you, and for an amazing education, and to further your career, but I'm telling you, you will find a guy there—if you want to. Almost all of the single girls I knew in business school graduated not single.

I told my parents about my new Ann Arbor friends. My mom wanted to meet them. My dad told me I always managed to find the nicest friends. He always said that. I told them about the warm fleece socks and how cold it was in Ann Arbor. They knew. They watched the Weather Channel every day. I told them how I'd started taking hot baths and drinking warm milk before bed. I didn't tell them about Michelle or about the Ambien. I didn't want them to think that I was really messed up. I didn't want to scare them.

My dad told me that he started drinking warm milk before bed and it helped him, too. He always wore socks to bed—his rag wool ones from L.L.Bean, along with their flannel pajamas. I could picture him sitting alone at their antique kitchen table late at night with his milk in his mug, straight out of the built-in microwave. I hoped his thoughts weren't going to the same places mine were.

I continued to see Michelle. She asked me more questions. I found the beginnings of some answers. She helped me come up with a few scenarios. In some, my mom continued to take the medication and it continued to work. In others, she got sicker. We even talked about the possibility of her dying, which I would caveat with "way way way out in the future." We talked about Neil, my father, my brother, my aunt Jo, and my friends.

When I couldn't sleep at night, I played out a few of these scenarios in my head. I started to normalize them as best as I could, even the bad ones. And then I willed myself to stop running through the scenarios. I gave up kissing the picture. I drank my warm milk. I took a deep breath. I stayed in bed. I put on my warm fleece socks, and I fell asleep.

I Wore a Belt

to My Son's Bris

Whenever a group conversation pivots to the topic of pregnancy and baby weight, Kara jumps in to speak for me and report on my postpartum body situation. She exclaims, still with utter disbelief all these years later, "Rach wore a belt to her son's bris."

It's true. Eight days after I gave birth to my first child, I put on my favorite black prepregnancy wide-leg pants from Banana Republic and looped a belt through each and every belt hole. It was technically a scarf—an old French one that used to belong to my grandmother. I thought it was chic and sentimental. I was glad I wore it on the day my baby boy was circumcised and then put down for a well-deserved nap as friends and family ate bagels, nova, and whitefish in our kitchen.

I don't remember a lot about that traumatic (probably more so for my son than for me) day, but I do remember people remarking on how quickly I had lost the baby weight.

"How big was the baby?"

"Are those your real pants?"

"Wait. Are you wearing a belt?"

In retrospect, the belt was overkill. I could have gone with a long, flowy top and leggings to hide the fact that my postpartum body had bounced back to normal freakishly quickly. I hadn't noticed how rapidly I'd become skinny again.

The baby weight fell off freakishly fast because I was a freak. I was a brand-new, twenty-nine-year-old mother who was more concerned with the tumors growing inside my fifty-seven-year-old mother than I was with the growth chart of my brand-new baby. I didn't think too much about feeding schedules or nap schedules or even tummy time. I just fell into some kind of routine where I fed my baby when he cried, changed him when he cried again, and then waited for him to coo and smile at me.

I'm not a total freak, though. I have a heart. I fell in love with my baby boy from the moment the labor-and-delivery nurse put him on my naked chest to let us bond after I pushed him out of me in almost record time. Neil marveled at my maternal instincts. I did, too. The first diaper I ever changed in my whole life was my own baby's, but I somehow knew how to do it. It felt like the most natural thing in the world when my baby latched onto my breast to nurse. It did feel weird that I had a legitimate-size breast for the first time in my life. After my baby was born, I understood what it felt like to need a bra.

I liked being all alone with my baby during our middle-of-the-night feedings. I sat in the yellow Pottery Barn Kids rocker in the corner of his room as he nursed. I stared at his soft baby head, taking in his baby smell, which I believe, but can't say for sure, may be more addictive than crack. I glanced out the double set of windows in his room, wondering if we were the only two humans wide awake at 3:00 a.m. in our quiet suburban town.

When my son was three months old, I went back to work. I left him with a young, smiley, seemingly energetic and playful nanny. I checked her references but beyond that didn't think too much about the what-ifs that could happen while I left my brand-new baby with a brand-new stranger. I was more concerned with the what-ifs surrounding my mother's cancer.

I was a calm mother, I think, because I was a nervous daughter. I brought my baby over to my parents' house for dinner a few nights a week—those nights when Neil was working late or traveling or out to dinner with clients. I ate dinner at my parents' kitchen table in the same seat I used to sit in every night during the dinners of my childhood. My baby sat next to me in his bucket car seat, sometimes on my lap or sometimes on my father's lap. He rarely sat on my mother's lap. She didn't have the strength to pick him up. Much later on, I understood that she was scared to get too close to him. Somewhere deep down below her ever-optimistic attitude and bright, shiny smile, she knew how sick she really was. She knew she couldn't beat the cancer. She struggled between wanting to love my baby in the intense and instinctual way I knew she could and being too scared to love him in that way and then having to leave him much sooner than she ever could have imagined. She struggled with having to leave all of us. She said her own goodbyes in the best way she knew how. I'm not sure others knew when she was saying goodbye to them. I knew when she said it to me, though.

When she told me I was "too young to go through this"; when she told me, "Aunt Jo will take you shopping for fall clothes"; when she told me, "Don't get pregnant again so soon"; and when she told me to "go home and take care of the baby," I knew she was saying goodbye. I did the best I could to say goodbye back to her. I told her I loved her. I told her I was sorry for being a nightmare in eighth grade and after the boyfriend breakup in college and with the hormonal acne in New York. She told me I never was. I hugged her. I kissed her. I squeezed her hand. She squeezed mine back until she couldn't.

She died when my baby was nine months old. I asked Aunt Jo what she thought it felt like for my mom when she was dying. She told me that she thought my mom just felt really tired—so tired that all she could do was close her eyes. I hope Aunt Jo was right. I hope my mother didn't feel pain. I hope she didn't feel sad or scared.

I took my mother's advice. I went home to take care of my baby. I thought of another piece of advice that my friend Colleen from business school had given to me. Colleen was the first real-life friend I knew who had a real-life baby the year before I did. When I became pregnant, she told me to remember that the baby should fit into our lives. I liked that advice. It made sense to me, and it stuck with me way more than any advice about how to get rid of my baby's gas or how to get him to sleep through the night. I also realized that I had been following Colleen's advice all along.

My baby fit into our lives in a way that I never really saw coming but that was necessary. That first summer after my mother died, my baby played the role of the family therapy dog. We were all so sad, but then the baby smiled or clapped his hands or spit out his mushed-up peas and we laughed. He made us happy even when that was the last thing we wanted to be. I think he willed himself to crawl just to cheer my father up.

When I needed to be a grieving daughter and couldn't get it together to be the hands-on new mother I'd thought I would be, I kind of think my baby knew it. He found his place in my life. He took ridiculously long naps and didn't wake up until I was finished crying on the phone to one of my college girls or to Aunt Jo. He put his head on my shoulder just as a tear was about to roll down my cheek. He sat quietly in his stroller as I pushed him on extralong walks, talking to my dead mother sometimes in my head and sometimes out loud, when I was sure no one but my new baby could hear me.

I had another baby not too long after that summer. My second baby was a girl, and she arrived almost a month earlier than expected. I didn't wear a belt eight days after she was born, but I did manage to fit into my favorite pair of prepregnancy jeans when she was just two weeks old. But the hormonal acne reappeared on my chin during my pregnancy with her, and I couldn't take anything to make it better.

I wore those prepregnancy jeans to my baby boy turned toddler son's nursery school play, leaving my brand-new baby girl at home with our amazing baby nurse, whose instincts I trusted way more than I did mine. Very few people spoke to me or even said hello to me in the audience of the nursery school play. I later learned it was because they wondered if something bad had happened with my pregnancy. Had I ever had the new baby? Where was the new baby? And how did I fit into those jeans?

The night the amazing baby nurse left, I took an extended shower. As my tears mixed with the water dripping down from the giant showerhead meant to mimic a rain forest, I said, "What the fuck!" out loud, knowing that the bathroom fan would drown out my sounds to the rest of the world, which somehow seemed to be functioning quite well outside my head and my bathroom. *How can I be a mother to these kids without my own mother? How can they grow up not knowing her, and how can she not know them?* Both of my babies were already asleep for the night. It was only 7:30 p.m.

My college friends started having babies. So did Neil's friends. We got together with them in New York or at our house in the 'burbs for early dinners with the kids where we ordered in pizza and drank wine and put the babies to sleep in their bucket car seats. Sometimes we got babysitters and met them out in the city for late, adults-only dinners. Those felt really good, like coming home again.

Neil and I laughed with each other about those other parents who lived and died by their babies' nap schedules. We took copious notes in our heads so we could make fun of them and their stories of baby sleep coaches and videos on proper baby swaddling techniques. I was the mom who put her half-asleep baby daughter in her car seat without socks and in a wet diaper in the dead of the winter so I could pick up my son from nursery school. I was the mom who forgot to turn on the baby monitor. I was also the mom who hired a babysitter sight unseen to live with us for a week at our rented beach house so that Neil and I could grab real dinners during our vacation at restaurants that didn't have high chairs or children's menus.

Maybe I was selfish or stupid, but being one of those "take your shoes off in my house; don't wake the baby or look at him the wrong way or breathe on him" kind of parents just wasn't in the cards for me. Maybe it was losing my mom just as I became a new mom? Maybe it was the advice from Colleen? Maybe it was having Neil as a partner? Or maybe it just was what it was? Our kids fit into our lives.

Our children got bigger. They got more interesting. I know there are some people who would like nothing more than to stare at a baby all day, mesmerized by the rise and fall of her breath or marveling at his tucked-back baby earlobes or the furrow of his brow, but that was not I. It was not Neil, either. We are not baby people. We are kid people, real people, people. And as our kids turned into real people, we loved getting to know those people and figuring out who they were and who they were becoming. That's the point, I'm going to say, when I had to let go of Colleen's advice, or at least modify it. It was time for me to learn how to fit into my kids' lives.

I had my own ideas of who I thought my kids would be. Neil did, too. All parents do, and if they say they don't, they're lying to you, or perhaps, worse, to themselves. I broke out in a giant smile when random strangers told me that my children looked like me. I bought my kids hats and T-shirts from some of the schools I went to. I told them stories—some they were interested in, and some that bored the crap out of them—about what I used to do when I was their age. They remind me of me in many ways and of Neil in other ones. My daughter is super organized and also super chatty, just like I am. My son has the same dry sense of humor as Neil and is equally laid back.

But they are also their own people. Like all good twenty-first-century parents, we exposed them to soccer, basketball, tennis, golf, swimming, art, cooking, piano, karate, and, I'm pretty sure, the viola. Some things stuck. Some fell flat before takeoff. My kids will not be Olympic athletes, and probably not even college athletes. They will not play any instrument onstage at Carnegie Hall. Maybe they would have if only I'd put them on stricter nap schedules? I have heard every douche bag, "my kid is the greatest [insert activity du jour]" comment from even bigger douche bag parents on the sidelines of the soccer field and in the folding chairs of the elementary school gym at the holiday school chorus concert. I force a smile back while making a mental note never to make eye contact with that parent again.

Here's another piece of advice I've picked up along the way. This one is from my friend Lisa. She explained to me one morning over coffee, quite bluntly, "At some point, your kid is who your kid is." That was another Oprah "aha" moment for me. I keep that in my back pocket, along with another wise piece of parenting advice I picked up somewhere else, I'm not sure where: "Meet your kids where they are."

My kids are who they are. They are—and I am knocking on wood, shouting out "poo poo" and spitting, and saying some made-up Yiddish words to ward off evil spirits as I write this—good kids. They are happy. They laugh a lot. They make me laugh—really hard. They are good people. They are good friends. They put other people's needs ahead of theirs—not always, but enough. I could go on and on about the things I love about my kids, but I don't want to be one of those douche bag parents. They are not perfect. They are not the greatest. They mess up. I do, too—all the time. My kids are not who I thought they would be when I used to dress them up in baby Penn baseball hats, which I now understand is a douche bag parent thing to do. So was dressing them in smocked dresses and shirts with Peter Pan collars.

It may sound like a good idea to try to mold your kids into who you thought you wanted them to be, and to have them meet you where you are, but trust me, it's so not. It's so much better to see your kids for who they are—the good, the bad, and all that other crap—and then to get up off your ass, walk away from the perfect life plan you had for them, and meet them exactly where they are. Maybe that's on the couch on a Sunday afternoon, watching hour seven of an ESPN documentary. Or maybe it's hunched over your kitchen table, going on hour three of disgusting-cake decorating. Maybe it's in the emergency room one Mother's Day morning as you wait to get back X-rays of a potentially broken wrist when you were supposed to be relaxing at a fancy brunch out. Maybe it's touring a school you never considered a possibility for your child. Maybe it's watching your kid mess up in the school play, or never get a part in the play, or get cut from the basketball team—in the first round of cuts. Go there. I promise you that if that's where your kid is, it's better than being anyplace else.

There are surely places of the future where I will need to meet my kids that I can't even fathom right now. But what I know for sure—I know I'm doing a little much with the Oprah stuff, but there's a reason she's made a bazillion dollars telling people what to do—is that I will try in the best way I know how to meet my kids where they are, to be a part of their lives, just as they've done for me, whether consciously or not, when I've needed that most.

I don't wear belts anymore. Does anyone? Maybe cowboys and Elvis impersonators? I find them constricting and a little too blingy. The image of me with a scarf wrapped around my waist makes me question my past fashion judgment.

"I did what I did" when my kids were babies, which is what my aunt Linda, my dad's brother's wife, whom I consider another awesome friend, even though she's technically my aunt, says in lieu of "I did the best I could." I don't know if what I did was the best I could or if I did the right thing. I don't know if being a too-chill, not-worried-enough mom back when my kids were babies was a good thing. I tend to lean toward good because, as my mom used to say—and again, knock wood, poo-poo, spit, yada yada yada—"the proof is in the pudding." And that pudding—I'm talking about the kids, in case I've lost you—is what I want to be around most now more than anything. I want to be in their lives. And, miraculously, for this very brief, shining moment, it feels like they want to be in my life, too.

Hair Pulled Back in a Twilly

I don't like to wear my hair back. I like my hair down. I like it to frame my face and sometimes hide parts of it, like the acne on my chin and the freckles on my cheeks. I'm pretty good at wearing my hair down. It's easy for me to do with my blunt-cut, relatively straight, and, at long last, thanks to postpregnancy hormones, thick hair. I wash my hair at night, go to sleep with it wet, and then run a flatiron through it the next morning.

My mother loved my hair pulled back.

"Why don't you pull your hair back so I can see your pretty face?" she asked me before I left for school in the morning, before I went out for a party at night, and really before I went out for anything. She called me one night during the final season of *Sex and the City* just to tell me how pretty Sarah Jessica Parker looked with her hair pulled back when she went out to dinner with Baryshnikov in Paris. She thought I should wear my hair back for my brother Jonny's upcoming wedding. I couldn't believe that was what she was thinking about then. She was quite sick during the last season of *Sex and the City*. I'm not sure why, but that final season of that show is still a reference point for my mother's cancer. So is Jonny's wedding. I told my mother I'd take her suggestion under consideration.

I wore my hair pulled back to my mother's funeral, just a few months after my brother's wedding and after the *Sex and the City* series finale. I did it in part because I knew that was how she liked it, even though I kept telling myself she wouldn't actually be at the funeral. I also did it because I didn't have the time or motivation to run a flatiron through my hair the morning of the funeral. I gathered my hair back with my fingers into a ponytail and wrapped around it a CVS hairband, which I grabbed from the giant stack of ponytail holders in my bathroom vanity drawer. I noticed a light purple silk hair ribbon in the drawer. It was pretty and also brand new.

Neil had bought it for me only a couple weeks before my mother died, when he was traveling for work in Paris. That trip was nothing like Sarah Jessica Parker's and Baryshnikov's. Neil was in Paris for just forty-eight hours, holed up in a conference room at a client's office for most of the time. He did manage to sneak out in my favorite European city to buy me something. He wanted to cheer me up. Everyone did then. My best friend from camp, Liza, flew down from Boston to spend time with me while Neil was away. I think she also flew down to say goodbye to my mom. Neil went to Hermès—fancy, I know—and bought me what I suspect was the least expensive thing for sale at the iconic French boutique. He bought me the light purple hair ribbon with the Hermès logo printed all over it in a beautiful and elegant design. "It's a twilly," he told me when I opened the Hermès orange gift box held together by the Hermès brown grosgrain ribbon. "Or at least that's what the fancy French lady told me it was called," he explained. We joked around, remembering when Tony Soprano gave Carmela an Hermès scarf, calling it "Hermeeze" and assuring her, "It's the best." Neil managed to make me laugh when he said those exact lines in his best New Jersey Mafioso accent. It was a twilly. I had seen one or two before. My fashion-forward friend Lauren used to wear one tied to the handle of her pocketbook, and my fashion-forward aunt Jo had worn one to tie back her own hair. I thanked Neil for my twilly and hugged him for an extralong time, recognizing how happy I was that he was back with me but also how sad I was that my mom would soon be leaving me. That's what it felt like: that she was leaving me and she was never coming back.

I wrapped my funeral ponytail in the twilly that funeral morning. It added much-needed color to my funeral outfit—a black silk blouse and short black A-line skirt. I thought my mom would have liked the splash of color in my pulled-back hair.

The twilly stayed tightly tied onto my ponytail at the funeral as I stood up on the bimah next to my brother at the synagogue where I had grown up. Both my parents had grown up there, too, and so had my grandmother. The ends of my twilly gently rotated up and down as I looked down at the printout of the eulogy that my mother had requested I write, and then back again at the massive crowd of people sitting out in the sanctuary in front of me. My mother asked me to write her eulogy about a month before the funeral, as I sat beside her after she had her last treatment at the hospital. Her oncologist had just told her that he didn't think there was anything else they could do for her.

"Rach, I want you to write my eulogy," she said, and then gave me her cute sad face, the same one she used to give me when I was a child and things didn't quite go my way. I told her yes, with a nod. And then she smiled and told me not to say anything about how sick she was when I went to Penny's wedding in Boston that weekend.

"This is Penny's day," she said. "Don't mention me. If people ask how I'm doing, just say 'fine.'"

I couldn't believe what she was telling me. I couldn't believe she was thinking about my friend Penny, about a wedding and a weekend in Boston that felt about a million miles away from the Philadelphia hospital room we were in. I said yes again, with a nod, half a smile, and a squeeze of her hand. And I kept my nonverbal promise to my mom that weekend. Everyone I spoke to at Penny's wedding asked about my mom. I told each and every one of them that she was fine, just fine.

When Penny greeted Aunt Jo in the receiving line right before my mother's funeral service, Aunt Jo whispered loudly in her ear, "I heard you were a beautiful bride." I was standing close enough to Penny and to Aunt Jo's loud whisper that I heard it. I didn't understand how anyone could be talking about anything else besides my dead mother in the coffin at the front of the synagogue. I was not comprehending the concept of a life that could be lived without my mother, an Earth that could spin without her on it.

I don't remember as much as I should about the funeral. I remember the twilly. I remember that I had never seen the synagogue that packed, ever—not even on the High Holidays. I remember looking out to the seats below me and above me on the balcony and seeing people standing at the back of the sanctuary, behind the filled seats. I had never seen the balcony full. I had been up there only once, when I was messing around with my friends one Sunday morning during religious school in fifth grade. My family always sat in the second row at synagogue. Those were our seats.

I don't remember talking to most of the people who packed the synagogue that day. I do remember feeling overwhelmed by the sheer amount of them. My giant extended family was there. Our giant circle of friends was there. A lot of friends of friends were there, too. And then there were people I saw there whom I hadn't expected to see. I saw my parents' gardener there. He always liked my mom. I saw the lady who owned the store in town where Neil had bought me the funky Chan Luu earrings. She really liked my mom, too. I saw my friend Colleen from business school, and also Shane. Neither of them had ever met my mom. But they showed up. So did my former Time Inc. coworker-friend Lisa. She had never met my mom, either. But she showed up. The partners in Jonny's law office showed up. My camp friends' parents showed up. My father's college roommate showed up. My old rabbi showed up. My cousin's father-in-law showed up.

I think about those unexpected show-ups every once in a while. I think about them when I hear that someone I knew, or kind of knew, has died. I think of them when I consider going to a funeral of that person I knew or kind of knew. And then I go. I show up. That's another good piece of advice I try to keep in my back pocket: When someone dies, even if you didn't know them that well, and even if you think it might be weird if you showed up at their funeral, it's not. Go. Show up. It's important. It's not weird. It will be appreciated and remembered.

My therapist Nora showed up. I starting seeing Nora soon after my baby was born, when my mother's tumors were growing and her lifespan was shrinking. Like Michelle in Michigan, Nora in Pennsylvania asked me a lot of questions. She let me figure out in my own time that the inevitable was coming. I cried a lot in her office. I sat on an oversize brown leather couch and made sure the square box of tissues on the side table next to me was never too far out of reach. Nora knew my mom outside her practice. She was a family friend of sorts. I asked her if it was okay for her to see me as a patient because of our already established relationship. She said it was. I was glad she did. I trusted her. My mother did, too, and I think it comforted her to know that I had someone I could "talk to." My mother asked me a few times about my sessions with Nora. I was usually pretty vague but told her that they were helpful. They were. I never told my mom about Michelle in Ann Arbor. I think I eventually I told my dad.

I sat on Nora's oversize couch just about a week after my mother's funeral. As I sank deeper into the leather cushions, I felt, for the first time in a long time, like I could breathe again. It occurred to me then, on Nora's couch, that I had been walking around in a world without my mother in it for almost a week. Somehow the earth turned. Life went on.

Nora asked me about the funeral. She asked me about writing the eulogy. Had it been helpful? Was I glad I did it? Was it hard to write? Was it scary to get up there and speak that day? I told her I didn't really remember much about it. I told her I was glad that Jonny was standing next to me, that it helped when he squeezed my hand that was hidden behind the lectern, especially when my voice started to crack. I was also glad that he agreed to read his part of the eulogy that I had written for him. Jonny and I got into a fight the night before the funeral as we reviewed our parts of the eulogy, practicing out loud in my childhood bedroom as friends and family ate filet and roasted potatoes brought over by family friends in the kitchen down below us. I can't quite remember the crux of the fight. Maybe he wanted to edit what I had written? Or maybe he wanted to say more or less of the part I assigned to him? I do clearly remember holding on to each word I had typed out like it was holy scripture—like I was still holding on to a piece of my mother in each of the words on the printed-out and marked-up computer paper.

It seems so trivial now. It also seems so obvious to me now that this fight came out of both of us not being able to deal with losing our mother way before we were ready to say goodbye. At the time I remember feeling like my loss hurt more than his—or really more than anyone's. Maybe he felt the same way? Maybe it was sibling rivalry at its worst—like when Jonny was in fifth grade and I was in fourth grade and he told me that fifth grade was way harder than fourth grade because of the teacher he had? Or maybe it was like when he went to law school and told me that law school was so much harder than business school?

In the years since my mother's death, Jonny and I haven't always been on the same page about the best way to miss her, the best way to incorporate her memory into our lives, or the best way to deal with our father. When we are having one of these not-on-the-same-page moments, I try to remember what it felt like when he held my hand on the bimah at the funeral or when he yelled "love ya, pal" across campus at the prep school, and then I remember that at his core, Jonny may just be the sweetest and most encouraging person I have ever met when he wants to be. I need to remind myself and perhaps him of that more often than not.

Nora told me that she couldn't see that Jonny was holding my hand. She hadn't noticed that my voice had cracked either. She said she'd been able to see that I was in the moment up there, giving the eulogy, that I was thinking and even feeling what I was saying. She was proud of me for doing that. She thought that was good for me.

I remembered having seen Nora at the funeral in the back left part of the main sanctuary. She'd been sitting next to someone I hadn't recognized, and she'd been wearing big glasses—not the smaller ones she usually wore during our sessions. I told her how nice it was that she'd come to the funeral.

She started to tell me about what she was thinking about when I gave the eulogy. I sat up straight in the cozy couch. Hearing a therapist's thoughts, her own point of view, intrigued me. It was like getting the answers to a test right after you took it and comparing your own answers in your head to the right ones.

"I noticed the pink ribbon in your hair," said Nora. *It was a twilly, a light purple one.* I didn't correct her. "I was thinking about a mother brushing her daughter's hair and putting a beautiful ribbon in her hair, maybe even braiding it. It struck me as a really beautiful thing. I'm not sure why, but it did," she explained.

That was deep and a little out there. I wasn't expecting that. I smiled at Nora, and then I got a little teary. We talked about who that mother was, who that daughter was. Was it my mom? Was it me? Was it a future daughter of mine? Was it no one at all—just a passing, nonsensical thought? I didn't know. Nora didn't either. The line between therapist to patient and friend to friend became a bit blurry that day. Nora knew more about my mom than Michelle, the Ann Arbor therapist, ever knew, and she knew more about me, too. She told me how proud of me my mom always was, how proud she would have been of me on the day of the funeral. We talked about how she would miss so much of my life. It wasn't fair. Life isn't fair. But in some small way, she suggested, maybe my mother would be with me throughout my life. Was I willing to consider that? I didn't know.

I stopped seeing Nora a few months after my mom died. I haven't seen a therapist since then, unless you count my phone calls with my college friend–therapist, Jill, and the Oprah podcasts I listen to. (I don't.) I'm not opposed to going to therapy again. I just haven't felt the need for it. I still think about Nora. And when I think of her, I think of my twilly, of the hair ribbon and the imaginary mother brushing her imaginary daughter's hair. I think that mother was my own mother. I think that daughter was me. I think Nora was telling me, or trying to get me to tell myself, that my mother will always be with me.

As I write this, it's been almost fifteen years since my mother's funeral. I still have the twilly. I actually have a couple more, which Neil bought for me in Paris when he went back to see that same client again. I wear them every once in a while, but never to funerals—more out casually at night, with a cute blouse and jeans. Sometimes when I tie my hair back in one of them, I tell myself that I'm too old to be wearing a hair ribbon in a ponytail. *Who do I think I am?* I ask myself. *Alice in Wonderland? Mary Ann from* Gilligan's Island? I usually hear my mother's voice in my head, ready and waiting with an answer. She tells me I look pretty with my hair pulled back, that I'm pretty, that the twilly is adorable, that it adds color and is very chic. She says I should keep it in. And so I do. And somehow I know my mother is with me and that she always will be.

Indoor Scarves and

How I Became a Writer

I can't say for certain that there's a correlation between the time I started wearing indoor scarves and the time I started to write professionally, but I think there might be. College friend Kara bought me my first indoor scarf for my thirty-fifth birthday and gave it to me at a surprise dinner that Neil threw for my college girls and their husbands and me. The scarf was from Anthropologie, which some people may know as a women's clothing, accessories, and home-goods store with a bohemian vibe, but for me, it's more than that. Anthropologie is a sacred place, a movement, a way of life. It's where I go to reward myself after a hard day of work or to cheer myself up when nothing else will do the trick. I feel better about my whole life when I walk into any Anthropologie store, whether the small one in my own suburban town, the big one in Rockefeller Center, or the medium-size one on the Third Street Promenade in Santa Monica. Every store has the same intoxicating smell, which seems to me to be a combination of fresh linens drying outside in the French countryside, yellow tulips on the countertop of a sunlight-infused kitchen, and steaming, dark hot chocolate from my favorite little café in the Kings Cross train station in London.

I walk through every Anthro store paying as much attention to the oversize embroidered cardigans and whimsical flowered blouses as I did when I looked up at the ceiling of the Sistine Chapel while touring Vatican City with my college girls Jill and Tracy during our junior year abroad. I always leave an Anthro store with more merchandise than I intended to buy, but also with the feeling that all my dreams will come true and that world peace seems doable. Neil knows how I feel about Anthro, as much as anyone who has never felt the pure joy of wearing one of the store's baby-doll dresses, tasseled earrings, or indoor scarves can. Anthro is his go-to place for last-minute, there's-no-way-I'll-screw-this-up gifts for me. The store managers at the Anthro in my town and at the one in downtown Philadelphia near his office know Neil. I'm pretty sure the manager in the Princeton Anthro knows my brother, Jonny, or at least she recognizes his face, from his frequent gift card purchases for me. Kara knew she picked a winner when she purchased my first indoor scarf at her local Anthropologie in the Westchester Mall in White Plains, New York.

Kara was the first person I knew who wore cozy, soft scarves indoors all day long. I'm not talking about the fancy, stuffy silk ones that my seventh-grade French teacher wore tied around her neck in a noose. Kara has been wearing indoor scarves with interesting colors and even more interesting fabrics on top of her sweaters, flannel shirts, and T-shirts since about 2002. She's quite the visionary, and she introduced me to the world of these life-changing accessories with the Anthro indoor birthday scarf. It's very shabby chic with an Indian tapestry pattern made up of raspberries, navy blues, and deep oranges, and it has matching multicolored fringe at each end. It's very me. Although, to be fair, *every* item at Anthro, except for the black velvet tube tops and white faux-fur vests, feels very me.

Back to the bigger question at hand: The year I turned thirty-five—a.k.a. the year of the indoor scarf—was also the year that I left my job in marketing to pursue a career in writing. Coincidence? Hard to say.

I've always enjoyed writing, and I received a lot of positive feedback on my writing skills in my preprofessional writing life. I liked writing papers in high school and college way more than studying for and then taking tests. I took pride in putting together a solid thesis statement, supporting evidence in body paragraphs, and then, of course, the concluding paragraph, which really, let's face it, is just a restatement of the intro/thesis paragraph. Once I figured out this formula, I rocked it—on analyses of literature in English classes and wars and treaties in American history classes.

I wrote in my marketing jobs. I wrote research reports, quarterly budget reconciliations, and future-budget plans like nobody's business. My writing work told a good story, in the kind of way in which a budget plan can tell a good story. But it felt a bit forced, a little too formulaic.

After my mom died, I started writing in a journal. My therapist Nora suggested I do this. She thought it would help me gather my thoughts and memories of my mother in some coherent way and hopefully allow me to move on with my life. I wrote late at night after Neil and my baby had gone to sleep. The words flew out of my brain and onto paper, and there was nothing formulaic about them. As I wrote, I realized that so many of my most favorite memories of my mom were from the times we shopped together. I focused more and more on the shopping together. I found my thesis, my supporting evidence, my body paragraphs, and my conclusion. The journal turned into a book. The book got published and reviewed and picked up in the press.

An editor from one of the papers that covered the book called me up one day on my cell phone while I was working at my day job in marketing. He told me he liked my writing style from the book and had a story he wanted me to cover. Would I be willing to cover it? *Cover it?* I imagined myself running up to an important-looking person speaking to a crowd in a park or in a giant lecture hall and shoving a Dictaphone in his face, asking for a comment, on what issue, I wasn't clear.

"Sure," I said into my not-yet-smart phone, a bit unsure of what I was getting into. "I can do it." He gave me the details. I was to show up to a panel discussion on "teenagers and sex," run by local experts at a nearby community building. He gave me the address, the date and time, and brief bios of the speakers. I took copious notes on the back of the printed-out PowerPoint presentation I was reviewing that day in my office. I could make this work. The panel was at night, so I could get there after my day job, after Neil was home, and after my baby was asleep. I wasn't sure why I wanted to try to make it work, but I did. I was excited—until the editor on the phone asked me for my Social Security number. I got a pit in my stomach and thought about ending the conversation. Was this some kind of scam? I knew not to give out secure information like a Social Security number over the phone—especially a cell phone. My father once made me call him from a landline at a Brooks Brothers store when I was there picking out a gift for Neil. I had first called him from my cell phone at his favorite preppy men's store to see if he wanted me to pick up anything for him. He did, and he insisted on giving me his credit card number so I wouldn't have to pay for his clothes. "But not over the cell phone, Rach. That's not secure," he said, quite sure of himself. "Call me back from a landline." I actually did.

"Why do you need my Social Security number?" I asked the suddenly sketchy editor, as I wondered what Big Brother–type character was tapping our call.

"It's for tax purposes," he said. "So we can pay you."

Pay me? It hadn't occurred to me that someone would pay me real money to write something for him—that this could be or could turn into a real job. I gave him my Social Security number, hung up the phone, and gave myself a little high five into the empty space in front of me.

My first assignment went well. I went to Staples and bought a Dictaphone and kept it on as the panelists spoke at the community building. I interviewed several panelists one-on-one after the official discussion ended. I stayed up really late writing that first article. I loved putting the words together to tell a story. The paper ran the story. The editor assigned me more stories. I covered local entrepreneurs, authors, speakers, weddings, fashion, and more panels, on health care, aging, and women's issues. They paid me. Then they paid me more. I started waking up really early to write at my laptop, either at the kitchen table or at my grandfather's antique rolltop desk in the corner of my living room. I usually had a cup of coffee next to my laptop, and I always had an indoor scarf wrapped around my neck—either the one from Kara or one of a few others that I had purchased for myself at my sacred happy place, Anthropologie.

A few months into covering other people's stories, I pitched my editor a personal-essay idea I had. I wrote it. He accepted it. I wrote that first essay one very late night when my house was finally quiet. I thought about that essay all day long while working at my real office, taking notes on scraps of computer paper in between meetings. I couldn't wait until nighttime so I could sit down and write.

A friend of mine in PR pitched my book to more media outlets. I appeared on television, and I wanted to wear an indoor scarf on camera, but the producer suggested I take it off. I did, but I put it back on right after the interview. A pretty well-known online magazine asked me to write for it. I said yes. Another friend of mine in PR asked me to write press releases for her clients. I said yes.

I gave up my marketing job. There weren't enough hours in the day for me to work in my office and write for the publications and the clients. And all I wanted to do was write. When I wasn't writing, I was thinking about when I could carve out time to write. And I was happiest when I could finally sit down at my laptop and write—while wearing, of course, one of my indoor scarves. I felt naked without one. I wrote a children's book, which got published, and then another, nonchildren's book, which also got published. It may sound like it was super easy for me to make a go out of writing, but it wasn't. I don't think it's easy for anyone to give up something safe in order to pursue a passion, but for me, it was worth it. I worked my ass off to produce, edit, and pitch, and then edit and edit again, the articles, the essays, and the books. But honestly—I know I sound like one of those really douchey people who use words like *charming* and *delightful* to describe a small town or a restaurant—it never really felt like work. All I wanted to do was write.

My most favorite place to be in the world, except for wherever Neil and my kids were and the rest of my family and my college girls and all my charming and delightful friends, was sitting hunched over my laptop at my grandfather's desk in that corner of my living room, which, I announced to my family, should be called my office. A giant cup of coffee was usually beside me, and an even more giant, although still super cozy and chic, indoor scarf was wrapped around my neck. Neil makes fun of me all the time for my scarfing habits. I wear scarves indoors almost every day—even in the summer. The summer scarves tend to be really thin and light in color and feel more to me like really big necklaces. I play with my indoor scarves a lot, pulling them in tighter in a moment of pause as I try to formulate my next thought, my next word, my next sentence, my next story or essay or book.

I've written personal essays, observational essays, short narrative pieces, long narrative pieces, creative nonfiction, and lots of other fancy made-up words that really are just bookends used to package the thoughts that come out of my head every day onto paper. People ask me how I come up with new ideas to write about. I don't have a great answer for them. It seems like the more I write, the more I have to write about. I keep notebooks all around my house, in my bag, and even in my car. I often carry my laptop with me. I write at Starbucks and a couple independent coffee shops in my town, which I would like to support more, but whose lattes I believe can't compete with Starbucks lattes. I always wear a scarf when I write at the coffeehouses. They're usually cold inside.

I surprise myself sometimes with the ideas that come out of my head. And I get really nervous every time I submit an idea, an essay, or any kind of pitch to any kind of publication. I read my pitch over and over and over again, and then I will myself to hit SEND to the submissions editor just when I feel like I might throw up if I have to read one of my words over again for the nineteenth time. I wonder if the pitching nerves will ever subside.

I am used to not hearing back from submissions editors. I am used to getting rejected. But I am starting to get used to having my pieces accepted. When the email comes back with a nod that says yes, we are going to run your piece, I sometimes look over my shoulder, searching for the real writer in the room. I suffer from impostor syndrome. It's a chronic condition. I'm waiting for my readers to step behind the curtain and see that it's just little old me, hunched over my laptop, wrapped up in a cozy indoor scarf.

I had a moment at my twentieth college reunion in 2016. An old classmate of mine told me she had read a few of my pieces in the *Huffington Post*. She had also bought my children's book for her daughter. It had become one of her daughter's favorite books. She thought it was so cool that I was a writer. *A writer? Who, me? I'm just a girl with an MBA who used to work in marketing and now sips coffee in front of my laptop while wearing a scarf.* That was my gut reaction. Before I could respond, my college girl Tracy jumped in to say that her kids love my children's book, too, and that yes, I'm a great writer. *I'm a writer. I'm a writer.* I practice saying that to myself in a loud whisper.

My kids tell people that their mom is an author, which sounds even crazier to me. They still talk about the day I visited their elementary school in 2012 to read my children's book as a "visiting author." I like that they remember that day. I also like it when my son walks in the door from school just as I'm closing up my laptop and asks me, "How many pages did you write today, Mom?" I like that he can relate, or at least connect, to my work. I use this as leverage for when he and his sister complain to me about the five-paragraph essays they have to write for school.

"I can bang that out in an hour," I tell them, as they roll their eyes at me. Our moment of connection is over. They make fun of me for wearing scarves indoors, too, especially when it's seventy degrees outside.

I think what I love most about writing professionally is the connections I've made with complete strangers. I've received emails from people who have read my books or my essays, and they sometimes tell me that my writing has touched them, that it has helped them through a tough time. No one ever told me that my budget estimates touched them.

My grown-up mom friend Melanie used to work as a social worker at the local chapter of a national cancer support community. I became a member of the community after my mother died. Melanie thought it would be a good idea, and I agreed to it because she did my initial intake into a club that "no one wants to be a member of." It's called Gilda's Club and was founded by Gilda Radner's husband, Gene Wilder, and her therapist, Joanna Bull, after Gilda died way too young from ovarian cancer. Gilda came up with that line about a club no one wants to be a member of.

I liked going to Gilda's Club. I liked talking to Melanie there and meeting her work friends and the nice lady volunteers who handed out free donated Starbucks. Melanie asked me if I wanted to lead a workshop at Gilda's Club about journaling and the power of writing to heal. I said yes. I put together a workshop that involved my reading out loud from my own journals to Gilda's Club members. These members were cancer patients or survivors or had lost loved ones to cancer. I talked to them about how to journal and, in the process, how to heal. The members wrote and showed me their work. I helped them edit it. They thanked me. I thanked them more. I thanked Melanie, too. I still do. I still show her rough drafts of my writing when we meet for coffee and wonder together how I became a writer, *a real writer*. Of course I wear an indoor scarf to our coffee dates.

My neighbor is an artist who teaches art classes in schools that can't afford art programming. She asked me if I'd be willing to teach a course on literary art in the schools. I said yes. I've taught writing workshops in schools where the only time the kids get to write is with a visiting "artist" like me. Some of the classrooms I've visited don't have overhead projectors or computers, and so I sit down on the rug with the students and we write together on paper, with our pencils. One student asked me to come back the next week to write with him some more. I wish I could have, but his school didn't have the time or budget allocated for more writing programming. I still think about that student, a lot.

Writing can be, and very often is for me, quite solitary, as I sit at my desk or at my kitchen table, wearing my indoor scarf all day and sometimes into the night, by myself. The solitude makes me treasure all the more the connections I've made through writing. When I'm going on hour five with just my coffee and my scarf, I think about my readers and my students. They make for good company in my head.

I can't think of anything I'd rather be doing than writing. So I don't. I hunch over my computer—I have terrible posture—and the thoughts continue to roll out of my head, into my fingers, onto my keyboard, and they begin to take shape. And I write and I write and I write some more.

Hamsa *Bracelets, Yoga,*

and Other Spiritual Stuff

I started seriously doing (I mean practicing) yoga in 2011, after I quit my gym. When I sat down and did the math, I realized that the gym was way too expensive for what I was getting out of it, which was basically thirty minutes on the elliptical machine a couple times a week, followed by drinking a large smoothie at the gym snack bar, which, as it turned out, contained more calories than I ever burned on the elliptical.

I knew that yoga could be a really good workout and that I could sweat a lot in a yoga class, even though it wasn't the old half-hour, less-than-three-quarters-of-a-smoothie calorie burn I had become accustomed to. At a yoga studio in town, I tried out a few power yoga—or, as we yogis in the know say, vinyasa flow—classes in between my kids' school drop-offs and my writing deadlines. I liked the classes. I liked them in spite, or perhaps precisely because, of the fact that I could barely walk two days after I finished my first real, hard-core power flow class. I had soreness in parts of my body where I didn't know muscles existed, like right below my hips and just above my wrists. No amount of time on an elliptical machine had ever made me feel that sore—in a really good way.

After a few months of dedicated (that's a very yogi thing to say) practice, I could see and feel my muscles getting stronger and my body looking toned. Neil noticed, too. He said my ass looked good. No one, and I mean no one, had ever told me that my ass looked good. I've always had a pretty flat stomach, but I inherited a lovely pear-shaped ass from my mother and every other Jewish woman in my family who came before her; that, plus my flat chest from my father's mother, makes me feel like I deserve my flat stomach.

But then yoga showed up and changed the shape of my ass, even with my pear-shaped-Jewish-lady genes and after all my years of sitting on it for super-long stretches of time. I told myself that I could put up with all the spiritual stuff that went along with yoga, as long as people (okay, it was one person, and it was my husband) told me that my ass looked good.

I was not into the spiritual stuff—at all. During the opening meditation, before the work-your-ass-off part of class began, I sat silent as the teacher and other students chanted, "Om, om, shanti, om," and sometimes some Sanskrit song that sounded a little bit like the Hebrew "I'm sorry for all the bad stuff I did this year" prayer I sing during Yom Kippur services, but much more spiritual. Sometimes the teacher accompanied the spiritual chants with her fancy yoga accordion, which I'm sure has a Sanskrit name that I can't remember, or just choose not to. On occasion, when I was feeling a little brave, I hummed along, trying to blend with the chanters, like I sometimes do at live concerts when everyone else knows the words to the songs except for me. When we lay down on our backs at the end of class during the closing guided meditation, I used that time wisely to review my grocery list in my head or test myself on my favorite girl and then boy names in alphabetical order.

I became a regular at my yoga studio, attending classes several times a week and waking up extra early on the weekends to get to class and back home again before anyone else in my house woke up. I started showing up to class ahead of time so that I could get a good spot, not too close to the front of the room, but close enough that I could see what the teacher was doing and follow her lead. I also found myself wanting to sit near the other regular students whom I recognized and wanted to get to know. I eavesdropped on their preclass chats over ginger Yogi Tea and was surprised to learn that they were civilians, regular people—just like I was.

They weren't born with their loose, natural, long, braided hair, their cool yoga tattoos, their *hamsa* bracelets and Buddha necklaces. Some of them told me how they came to class to tone their asses, their thighs, or their upper arms. Others came to relax and meditate or stretch out after running or biking, or to heal an old sports-related injury.

They told me about their lives outside yoga. They were moms, dads, doctors, nurses, hairdressers, teachers, artists, and even a couple writers. I told them about my life. We became friends—yoga friends. I got so excited when I saw one of my yoga friends outside the studio—kind of like when you're a kid and you see your teacher buying milk at the grocery store and you begin to understand that she's a regular person, too, just like you.

I also got to know (read: worship) my yoga teachers. I asked them a lot about how they got into yoga. One of my favorite teachers is a former aerobics instructor, and sometimes when I watch her teaching, as the light from the oversize front window in the studio hits her just so, I see an uncanny resemblance between her and my mother. I told her that, and she gave me a huge, warm, long yoga hug, which felt like sunshine and a full-body massage. Another awesome teacher used to dance professionally. She reminds me of a much younger version of my flat-chested grandmother, who, incidentally, practiced yoga long before I knew that yoga was something you could practice, lying on her back with her legs up the wall in her pajamas and her fancy old-lady silk robe every night before bed in her apartment in Boca Raton. She lived to be a healthy and vibrant ninety-three-year-old woman. I attribute some of that longevity to yoga.

My cousin Catherine, another civilian, not to mention former college athlete and lawyer, got really into yoga about the same time I did. Catherine got so into it that she enrolled in a yearlong teacher training course, which she likened in intensity to studying for the bar exam. She now teaches yoga at another studio, to kids after school and to adults at 6:00

a.m. before they go off to work, in an amazing sunrise vinyasa flow class. Catherine and I came out to each other, comparing notes on our favorite yoga poses, favorite yoga music, and favorite yoga pants. She likes lululemon; I prefer Gap Body. We also admitted to each other that we were starting to get into all the spiritual yoga stuff. We talked openly about Reiki vision boards, gratitude journals, and energy—and not the Thomas Edison kind.

Catherine wears all those cool yoga clothes, including super-soft tank tops that say PEACE, LOVE, NAMASTE and sweatshirts that say SPIRITUAL GANGSTER. She pairs them quite nicely with her *hamsa* bracelets, which she makes with her adorable daughters at her own kitchen table. I have a few *hamsa* bracelets. I love them. I wear them a lot, sometimes by themselves and sometimes stacked with my Buddha beaded bracelet or an antique gold bangle that used to belong to my grandmother. I'm pretty sure that the hand of God can go with anything.

I am told that the *hamsa* is a protective sign meant to bring happiness, luck, health, and good fortune to those who wear it. I'm open to that idea. I'm also open to the idea that it could just be a cute piece of jewelry that fits nicely on my skinny wrist. But the thing is, I feel really good when I wear my *hamsas*, my Buddhas, and my *mala* beads. Part of it is because Catherine made many of them, and I like the whole homemade, arts-and-crafts, camp vibe. Part of it is because they remind me of yoga and how much I love practicing it with my yoga friends and yoga teachers, who I like to think are my real friends. And I must admit, part of it is because I do feel like maybe, just maybe, I'm warding off evil spirits and exuding and attracting good energy when I wear them. Relax. Breathe. I'm not getting a yoga tattoo or a nose piercing, but I have come to believe, in a way that makes so much sense to me, in so much of the spiritual yogic stuff. At some point, though I'm not sure exactly when, my humming turned into full-on "om, shanti, om," sing-it-like-no-one's-listening chanting. Around that same time, my end-of-class grocery list review turned into actual, lie-there-and-breathe-and-let-the-thoughts-come-and-then-go meditation.

I have my own mantra. It's "let go," and I say it to myself over and over as I breathe in and out through my nose and chill the fuck out in a way that was never possible for me in my preyoga life. I've observed weird images running through my head—or, as we yogis say, my mind's eye—during meditation. I've seen all the colors of the rainbow; light blue rocky sand; giant orange ocean waves; fire-breathing dragons with distorted faces; magnolia trees in full bloom; and also the faces of real people from my past whom I have not thought of in years. *And then guess what?* I ran into a few of those people in the days and weeks that followed those meditations. Or, in some cases, those people called me or emailed me, or a friend of mine randomly asked me about them. Coincidence? Perhaps. Perhaps not.

Other weird things started happening to me during meditation. One day toward the end of class with my favorite teacher, who at that point I had convinced myself might be my mother reincarnated, I came to from the meditation with tears in my eyes as I felt a tingling sensation through my body. The Beatles' "Let It Be" played in the studio at that moment, and my teacher–reincarnated mom explained to the class that Paul McCartney wrote that song in tribute to his late "mother Mary" who "in times of trouble" gave Paul the advice "let it be." I never knew that. I really needed to hear that very same advice that morning as I was trying to figure out how to navigate some crazy family stuff going on in the wake of my mom's not being alive anymore to make everyone in my family happy or at least functional. And so I let it be. It helped.

I now look forward to savasana, corpse pose, as I take the time to channel certain images and thoughts in my head. I've imagined an older-lady version of my mom being a grandmother to my kids, giving them a hug, and telling me I'm doing "just fine" and to "let go." So, basically, my dead mother is speaking my mantra to me in my head. It's kind of crazy. But it works for me, and I feel so good after meditation. I sleep better at night, and I'm told that I'm a much nicer person after I practice yoga.

I judge people and places based on their energy and say things like, "I can't go there anymore—bad energy" and, "I want to hang out with her more. I love her energy." It turns out that the energy they talk about in yoga really is the Thomas Edison kind of energy after all. The CliffsNotes version of all four years of the science classes I took in high school: We are all made of atoms, which make up the cells in our bodies, and therefore we all have a certain amount of energy in our bodies. When we're feeling happy and good about ourselves, that energy is at a higher level, and when we're feeling really crappy, our energy levels drop. You know those bitchy girls who always complain and suck the life out of the party? They have really low energy. You could, if you were a yogi like I am, call them energy vampires, because that is a thing. I find myself being attracted to people with higher levels of energy, and I think/hope that I attract those kinds of people. It's like when you meet some guy who appears on the surface to be not all that attractive, but then you get to know him, and he's so funny and sweet and kind and always smiling that you decide he actually *is* pretty good-looking—that's his high level of positive energy. The same goes for the seemingly physically drop-dead-gorgeous girl who never smiles and is mean to everyone, even her super-sweet old grandmother. All of a sudden, the hot chick doesn't look so hot anymore because she's giving off negative, super-low levels of energy.

I'm a little scared of my energy levels and the powers they may be sending out into the universe. I think I might be a witch. There have been way too many times in my yoga-practicing life when I haven't felt like going out to an event or a party, and then it's turned out that one of my kids gets sick or the babysitter cancels, so I don't have to go. I've convinced myself that I am the catalyst for a few cases of strep throat, a couple of giant snowstorms, and our babysitter's car troubles. I can't control my witchcraft. Maybe wearing more *hamsa* bracelets would help? Maybe fewer? Not sure.

I do know that I'd like to continue to practice yoga for as long as I can. I aspire to be like the ninety-eight-year-old woman I read about in an Athleta catalog. She's been teaching and practicing yoga for seventy-five years. She looks better in her yoga pants—hers are Athleta, obviously—than most people I know, even those who are less than half her age. She rocks this long, funky necklace that looks like it's giving off high levels of positive energy, and of course she has a mantra.

My family encourages me to keep practicing my yoga. "Go to as many classes as you like," Neil tells me. "Go every day." I think he likes me better on the days I practice. I like myself better when I practice. And there's also my new and improved yoga ass, which counts for something for sure.

H Wraparound

and Dad

My childhood friend Stacey does this awesome, deadpan imitation of my dad. She sets it up like this:

"Here's my imitation of Jimmy when he's really happy for you: 'Hi, Rach.'

"And here's my imitation of Jimmy when he's really mad at you: 'Hi, Rach.'"

In both impersonations, Stacey uses the same "I might be half-dead, or maybe I'm just really stoned" monotone. That's my father—mellow yellow, even Steven. It's a shame there's not a good adjective that means "cool as a cat, nothing upsets me ever" and rhymes with Jimmy. My friend Amanda from high school calls my dad Steve because she thinks he looks exactly like Steve Martin, so there's that. I see the resemblance. The best nickname anyone ever gave my dad was Jimbo, which is now the first five letters of his email address. The last four letters are my son's nickname, which is kind of random, and when we ask him why he chose that email address, he says, "Why not?" Why not, indeed? That's another good Jimmy Levy line used to explain away a lot of "no big deal" or "whatever floats your boat" sentiments that my dad feels. Are you getting this? My father is extremely chill. It's a little scary to imagine him after a yoga class or a deep meditation. His pulse might stop.

My father's even-keeled nature, coupled with his eternally optimistic, "the glass is always half full" attitude, was a staple of my childhood. He had a few key pieces of advice that guided his life and that he passed on to Jonny and me: work hard, try your best, live below your means, never go to bed angry, never sue anyone, and always get along with everyone in your family. That was it—Jimmy's words of wisdom.

This advice was never far from me, and I always appreciated the solid relationship I had with my father, but still, he was my father—not my mother. He went to work and then came home to take a nap to mellow out even more. He came to my school plays, visited me at camp, cheered for my sports teams (not too loudly, of course), and, as I got older, inquired about the pressure of my tires and the RAM on my computer.

My mother was the one with whom I shared my secrets. She helped me through the trials and tribulations of childhood and adolescence. She was always there with the right tools and words to help heal my skinned knee or mend my broken heart. She taught me about manners and values and what to say and do and wear. She showed me by example what it meant to be a good friend and really a good person—a compassionate and contributing member of society. But then she died way before I ever fathomed she would. To say I felt lost without her would be a huge understatement.

In one of my "life's not fair—I still need a mother" tantrums, which I threw only in front of my mellow, "I can take anything you throw at me" father, he said to me that he could be "the mother and the father." He uttered these words in his cool-as-a-cucumber voice, accompanied by his ever-present smile and upbeat attitude, which I always wished that I could somehow bottle and sell. I would have made a fortune off it.

"You can't be the mother," I said to him not calmly at all, holding back angry tears, feeling more cheated than I imagined he could ever feel. "You're the father." I was sure he couldn't be the mother. I doubted he could even be the father. Right after my mother died, my father seemed to need me way more than I needed him. Like most widowers, or so I'm told, my father was clueless. He went to the grocery store and asked Murray, the store manager, where they kept the milk, as if he were walking into Brooks Brothers in search of a new sport jacket.

I became a personal concierge of sorts for my father, buying gifts on his behalf, picking out the enclosure cards, and filling them out, making sure to leave room for him to sign his name at the bottom. I accompanied him to his doctor's appointments, holding a copy of the list of the medicines he took and acting as "a second set of ears," as he would explain to the doctor *du jour*. He introduced me as his "boss," which he thought was cute, but which pissed me off. I didn't want to be his boss. I wanted him to be my boss. I wanted something out of him, something missing from the giant hole left by my mother's death.

In the last nearly decade and a half since my mother died, my father and I have spent more quality time together than we probably did in the nearly first three decades of my life, when she was alive. It's possible that I've had dinner with my father more as an adult than I did as a child. He has become, hands down, the biggest fan of my mediocre cooking, as he's always been easy to please in the food department, thanks in part to my mother's thirty-plus years of crappy cooking. He pays me huge compliments even when I serve him pasta with vodka sauce (from the jar) or his favorite item, which he incorrectly calls Chicken Rach—really just the frozen Mandarin Orange Chicken in a bag from Trader Joe's. He happily accepts the "cup of decaf" that I know to offer him after dinner. I've upgraded him in recent years from Sanka to Keurig and now to these fancy Nespresso decaf pods.

"Whoa!" he said the first time I made him a coffee from a Nespresso pod. "I feel like I'm at an Italian coffee bar." And then he smiled and may have winked at me, like my mother used to.

My father has done a lot of the things that my mother used to do with me when I was a child and probably some of the things she would have done if she had lived to see me through adulthood. He sometimes comes shopping with me and patiently waits outside the dressing room while I try on clothes, offering pretty sound advice on what looks good and what doesn't. He has always been generous with me in the gift-giving department, although he usually gets me things that he himself would use or wear—things like golf clubs, ski parkas, and collared tennis shirts that I would wear if I were Martina Navratilova and it was 1985.

When I turned forty, my father upped his game in a big way and bought me this awesome orange leather wraparound bracelet from Hermès. (Yes, that Hermeeze—the one they say is the best.) It's very modern, and there's just a tiny little H clasp that connects the leather pieces together like a mini-belt. It's not one of those obnoxious, "here's the name of the designer piece I way overpaid for" items that my mother always made fun of. When viewed from a distance, the H wraparound looks like a bunch of old fabric bracelets stacked together, sort of like the arts-and-crafts friendship bracelets my daughter wears on her wrist every summer when she returns home from camp. My father actually took the initiative and asked me what I wanted for my big birthday, and I used the opportunity to suggest the wrap bracelet, which I had admired in a fashion magazine. We picked out the bracelet together online. He took great pride in ordering it with just a few clicks as I stood over his shoulder at my laptop one night after his cup of decaf at my house. He was amazed at the whole online-shopping phenomenon. I assured him that the Hermès website was secure enough to take his American Express card.

I wore the H wraparound bracelet the night of my fortieth-birthday party, a casual house party that Neil threw one very cold and snowy January night. I got a ton of compliments on the bracelet at the party, and I proudly told each complimenter that the bracelet was from my dad. They were shocked.

"Your dad? Jimmy? Jimbo? Steve?" they asked, sometimes twice.

"I know. Can you believe it?" I replied, a little tipsy from the homemade party sangria.

"He's come a long way," I said to a few of my college friends and my grown-up mom friends at the party. He grocery-shops on his own, without the help of Murray or anyone else in the store. He cooks, too, on the stovetop and the grill (I'm not sure about his oven use). He goes to doctor's appointments by himself, having become his own advocate and his own second set of ears. He shops online (on secure sites only, of course), and he set up his iPad and his printer without calling me for help. I suspect he put in a few calls to a real-life person over at Apple HQ in Cupertino—not overseas—but that's acceptable to me.

It's taken me a while, but I've finally come to understand that his cluelessness and his helplessness stemmed from his own feelings of grief and sadness. I get it now. He, too, was lost right after my mother died.

I once asked him if he thought my mom knew how sick she really was.

"I think she did," he answered, without pausing to think about my question.

"Why do you think that?" I followed up.

"Because one night toward the end, she rolled over in the middle of the night in bed, put her arm around me, and said very softly, 'I'm going to miss you, Jimmy,'" he explained.

I cried when he told me that. He teared up. The image of that middle-of-the-night farewell to a loving husband of thirty-five-plus years still slays me. Life wasn't fair for him, either. He was cheated, too.

Like most youngish widowers, or so I'm told, my father dated. The ladies showed up pretty soon after my mother died with their briskets and their Bundt cakes and whatever other dishes it takes to catch a clueless widower. Although my father said he would never go out with anyone else when my mother was sick (I believe his exact words were "I'll be a monk"), he went out with them. I don't blame him. I never did. People close to me and some not so close to me have asked me over the years if it bothered me that he dated. It didn't—at all. I wanted him to find someone. I didn't want him to be lonely, and I definitely didn't want to make him Trader Joe's dinners and Nespresso-pod decaf at my kitchen table forever. I knew that no one would ever replace my mother, and I suspected he felt the same way.

I was told by those in the know that he was a good catch. He's tall, he has all his hair, and he drives at night. Apparently, when you're a youngish-old-man widower, that's all it takes. I also think his being a really nice, mellow, the-glass-is-always-half-full kind of guy, also helped. The women he "took out" all seemed quite nice. He brought some of them over to my house, I think because he didn't know what else to do with them and also because he wanted my opinion. I told him I liked each of them, even when I didn't.

My father eventually found someone special. He's not lonely anymore. I don't have to serve him Trader Joe's dinners at my kitchen table. His girlfriend—or, as my grandfather used to say when describing boys I dated, his "special friend"—is lovely, and I love her. She's actually awesome, but I feel like *lovely* is a word more apropos for a widow who goes steady with my widower father. And I'm not just saying that she's so awesome and lovely and that I love her because I inadvertently set her up with my father. The setup was a group effort between me, my grown-up mom friend Melanie, and her childhood friend Beth. We made the match through a group text and a few follow-up phone calls, until I finally decided to email my father his future girlfriend's digits. My dad and his girlfriend thank Melanie for the setup when they see her.

"It's the best thing we ever did," I say to Melanie when I forward her pictures of my dad and his girlfriend traveling together or out to dinner or just looking happy to be with each other.

They're living a good life together—one that my mother missed out on, but one that his girlfriend's late husband missed out on as well. I don't know if they talk about their late spouses with each other. I don't ask. It's none of my business.

His girlfriend reminds me of my mother in many ways, but she never tries to be her. She knows I'm not looking for another mother, and I know I'm not her daughter. My father says that his girlfriend and I "make a great team." I like it when he says that. It doesn't piss me off at all. Sometimes when I go on long walks by myself down by the canal on the towpath in my little suburban town, I talk to my mother and catch her up on our lives, explaining in some detail about what she's missed. I've told her about my writing career, my new grown-up mom friends, my kids (I go into great detail there), and even about my dad's girlfriend. I think she'd approve.

I often wonder what kind of grandmother my mother would have been. I think she would have been great, but the truth is, I'll never know. My father is an awesome grandfather. When he's in town, he's always there to babysit when I need him. He's met my kids off the school bus more times than I care to count when I get stuck somewhere or just need backup. And when he's with my kids, he's really with them—interested in all they have going on in their lives in a way I can't always be as I try to organize my house, finish my work, and get some kind of dinner on the table.

I'll admit that it did take me some time to feel comfortable with my father watching my kids. When they were babies, I saw him as a warm body—someone who could call the fire department if need be when they were asleep upstairs in their cribs. But he has proven himself to be much more than that. He talks to my kids a lot about life when he was growing up and when I was, too. He tells them about my mom sometimes, when he thinks I'm not listening, but I am. He tells them how she hated to cook, how she never let me chew gum when I was a kid, and how she had the cutest freckles, just like my daughter. My kids seem genuinely interested in his stories in a way I never could be and probably never will be. He plays board games and card games with them, and they teach him how to set up group texts and FaceTime without looking like a giant cyclops on his end of his iPhone.

My father has gotten to know my friends really well, and he hangs out with us sometimes, whether it's for a cup of coffee (obviously always decaf for him) or a visit at my house. He remembers key details about their lives, which always amazes me, and he's been known to get into some solid discussions with them.

My discussions with my father have gone to a whole new level in recent years—deeper than our very quick check-in talks in my childhood. We talk on the phone nearly every day. We tell each other our secrets, and every now and then he jokes to me that our conversation should remain "just between us girls."

High praise runs deep in my family. We are all famously overly generous with compliments, particularly my father. His kids can do no wrong in his eyes, and he's always more than happy to report to Jonny and me, "Everyone I run into says I have the best kids." I've heard some version of this report for most of my life. Jonny has too. I take this with a giant grain of salt, knowing full well how unlikely it is that any high-functioning adult would trash someone else's child in front of that kid's father.

I think it's cute. My father is proud of us—proud of whatever part he had in raising us. And here's the thing: I'm proud of him, too. And I'm proud of me. I raised a good father, or mother, or whatever it is that he has become to me.

Push Presents

and Mom Dating

Mom dating is a thing. It's like real dating—i.e., searching for a lifelong soul mate—but for me, at least, more painful than the latter.

When I moved to the suburbs, pregnant with my first child, I didn't think about the fact that I knew no one my age in my new neighborhood. I was more focused on the old red barn house that Neil and I had bought—the one with the two-car garage and open kitchen with room for three stools at the end of the counter. I imagined myself sipping coffee while sitting on a stool with my new baby in my lap, chatting away with my new best mom friend and her baby, who would become best baby friends with my baby. It looked like an awesome life in my head, but in reality, my other kitchen stools remained empty.

I missed my college girls, my business school girls, my childhood friends, my camp BFF, and my magazine work friends. I didn't appreciate how important these female connections were to me in my everyday life until they weren't there anymore, at least not physically. I was told I needed to find new friends, mom friends. But where would I find these new BFFs?

I heard whispers in the aisles of the grocery store and in the pediatrician's waiting room. "Take a music class, browse around the bookstore, or check out the baby gym." Apparently, there was an entire underground mom-friend pickup scene—like an after-hours club or something? I had no idea. They don't tell you that at your twenty-week ultrasound.

I signed up for a baby music class at the synagogue in town when my son was four months old. I still remember the carefully selected outfit I wore for the big day: tan low-rise corduroys, a black turtleneck sweater, and velvet ballet flats. I was way overdressed. Most of the moms wore sweats or jeans and sat cross-legged on the floor while they sang to their babies, laid out on fleece blankets in front of them. I noticed that a few of them were blinged out in jewelry announcing their new-mother status.

Around her neck, one mom wore a silver chain with two silver mini-kid cutouts hanging from it. Looking more closely, I noticed that one silver kid had a hair bow and the other, a sideways baseball cap. I got it. She had a boy and a girl, and she wore a tiny version of each on her neck—clever. Another music mom had two enamel pink ballet slipper charms encrusted in diamonds on a longish chain around her neck. Two girls equaled two ballet slippers. *What would a boy shoe charm be? A sneaker? A loafer?* A third mom had three gold disks hanging from a shorter chain around her neck. Each disk had one of her children's names engraved on it. This new-mom jewelry collection has a name. These pieces are called push presents, as in, "I pushed this baby out of my body, and so my spouse bought me a necklace with my baby's name on it in lieu of writing a thank-you note." Full disclosure: I have a push present. Actually, I have two, one for each of my children. I feel a little bad about the second one, since I didn't push my daughter out of me, like I did with my son. She was cut out from my abdomen in an emergency C-section because she was breach. Neil gave me two tiny, skinny eternity bands to thank me for pushing out/ getting his babies cut out of me. They're actually called micro bands. Kara and Penny have them, too.

I wear them stacked between my wedding ring and my engagement ring every day. They blend in and to me just look like pretty little rings with colorful stones in them. They don't have oversize charms of cutout little people or little people's shoes hanging off them. I never felt the urge to wear jewelry that announced to the world that I had pushed/had a baby cut out of me. I figured people would figure that out when they saw me carrying a baby in a car seat bucket, looking exhausted, clueless, and lonely.

The day of that first baby music class, I sat on the other side of the room, far away from the fleece blanket–toting, baby charm–wearing new moms. They didn't talk to me. They barely even looked at me. They weren't my people. I left the class without a phone number—not even one.

I signed up for a "moms' club" in my town. It was free to join. You just had to submit your email address and phone number on the bottom portion of a flyer, which promised "fun for moms and babies." I saw the flyer hanging on the bulletin board at my Starbucks. I went to one of the moms'-club meetings in the basement of a church in town, where there was a rather complicated craft project set up for the babies, who clearly couldn't use scissors or glue. I watched from a distance as the other new moms cut out pieces of felt and spread glitter on top of designs made from glue while their babies slept in their own car seat buckets and their push present charms of their miniature metallic babies dangled from their necklaces. I wondered if the charms would get caught in the glue. I twisted my own secret push present microband around my ring finger and watched from a safe distance, then promptly left the church basement alone, again. No digits.

Things only got worse after another local group of new moms stood me up at a Borders bookstore. Apparently, they changed the time at the last minute, but I never got the message. A friend of my mom's took pity on me and set me up with a random young mom whom she'd met at a baby shower. When I got the call about the setup, I could tell this one was a stretch.

"I think you'll hit it off. Her baby is only a week older than yours, and she's tall, just like you." *Really? Is this what it's come to? Dating boys was never this hard.*

I hit rock bottom when I found myself way too deep in the depths of an unhealthy relationship with one new mom. She picked me up at a time when I was feeling vulnerable, even a little desperate, and she was intense. I should have known she was a stalker when she asked for my number so quickly and then called me the same day we met.

After several rocky months of playdates, lunches, and even dinner with our husbands, the mom-dating equivalent of meeting the parents, I had to end it. I stopped calling, but she needed closure and confronted me to get it. It was a rough breakup.

I resigned myself to a life without mom friends. *I'll be okay*, I told myself. I had my real friends from other parts of my life, and although they didn't live nearby, they also didn't wear mini-versions of their kids around their necks, and I wasn't scared that they would stalk me and turn into bunny boilers.

It was when I finally stopped looking so hard that the mom-dating scene warmed up. It always happens that way. I first met Melanie, the social worker from Gilda's Club/ matchmaker for my dad at a brunch hosted by a woman we both knew in town. We bonded over our lives prekids, having both lived in New York City and having both stayed really close to our friends from college and other parts of our lives. When she asked about my family and I told her that my mother had recently died of cancer (something I didn't always love to share when meeting new people, as it often caused an awkward pause, followed by a forced "I'm sorry"), she nodded, as if to say of course we would meet and become friends, and then she told me about Gilda's Club. Melanie is a self-proclaimed witch like I am, possessing all the powerful energy vibes and such.

Sandy and Lisa, a couple of girls turned moms whom I knew from growing up in the area and who had moved back just like I had, called me to get together with our husbands soon after I had my first baby. I didn't know them that well when we were kids, because they were older than I was, but I remember worshipping them a bit from afar at different points in my childhood. I was so nervous on our first couple of dates, as I tried really hard to prove to them that I was worthy of being their mom friend and that I was no longer the shy little kid they used to babysit for. I guess I presented well. They called me again and again, and they've become awesome friends of mine. Lisa is one of the Lisas—not the one from the magazine company. She introduced me to yet another Lisa, who, as it turns out, I went to camp with. I was scared shitless of Camp Lisa when I was a kid because she had a reputation for being a badass at camp, but she's actually a really great person. She *is* kind of a badass, though, and I love her for that.

As my babies got older and became full-fledged kids, they made friends on their own in their classrooms, on their sports teams, and wherever else suburban kids meet their future lifelong BFFs. I met my kids' friends' moms, and then some of them became my friends, some more quickly, some more slowly, and some closer than others. My daughter is still really tight with a great group of girls she met in nursery school, and the moms of those girls are still tight with me. There are a couple repeat names in that group, too—two Randis and a few Staceys. I also have a small collection of Nancys and Allisons and a gaggle of Laurens/Loris/Lauras. No Jens, which is surprising, since I grew up with about a thousand Jens, Jennys, and Jennifers. None of my real mom friends wear bedazzled mini-kids on any part of their bodies. Some have stacked eternity bands on their fingers. I've admired them over the years.

We have known each other now for an actual legitimate amount of time, since our oldest kids are teenagers and our younger ones are almost there. I have this picture framed on a shelf in my kitchen, in front of a huge collection of cookbooks that I never use, and I smile whenever I see the image in passing. It's of me and a big group of my mom friends posing in front of a green screen, holding ridiculous props, like fake mustaches and pipes, oversize plastic glasses, and one of those Mardi Gras masks. It's from my son's bar mitzvah party. We were all a little drunk that night, but we have giant, genuine smiles on our faces in that photo. We look really happy to be together—to celebrate a kid we watched grow up together, one we drove in carpools, cheered for from the sidelines of the soccer fields, and sang "Happy Birthday" to one too many times over way too many sugary birthday cakes covered in candle wax and little-kid spit.

These mom friends of mine, they became my real friends. They are my people. They are as real as the college girls and the childhood friends and the like. Not that I rank them or anything, although Neil and I have established our own version of a birthday ranking game to amuse ourselves, wherein we rank those friends of ours who remember our birthdays in a way we feel is commensurate with our relationship to them.

I feel so lucky to have made meaningful and, I think/hope, lifelong connections with these mom-friend ladies. We have much more in common than just having had babies at around the same time and living in the same town. Like a fine wine, or so I'm told, these friendships have gotten better with age. They also took time to form. I couldn't force these women to appear in a baby music class amid a sea of fleece baby blankets and way-too-obvious-for-my-taste push presents.

We have our own histories, our own adventures, and our own stories to tell. We have seen each other at our best and our worst, like in the early morning at school drop-off, with no makeup and sometimes no bras, and also with makeup and our hair brushed or pulled back, on fun trips to the theater, to lunch, to the beach, and to the ski slopes.

They remind me of my mom's birthday group in that way, her gang of lifelong friends whom she met when she was a young mother. I wish she knew all my new mom friends, because I think she would love them all like I do. I talk about my mom to my mom friends, and a few of them have told me that they wish they had known my mom, but also that they feel like they do know her—through me. That makes me feel so good.

We celebrate holidays with many of them. We talk to each other about our extended families, our aging parents, our lives before kids, and our growing children, and also about changes in our careers, our marriages, and our friendships.

I occasionally see some of the old charm-wearing baby-music-class moms around town and even some of the ladies from the craft-making meeting in the basement of the church. They seem like nice people when I pass them in the narrow aisles at CVS or the car line at school pickup. Sometimes I smile at them or even say hello. Some of them recognize me. Others don't, or maybe they do and choose not to say hello, remembering what a miserable bitch I looked like back in the day.

It reminds me of college and how you become friends with everyone on your hallway during the first few weeks of freshman year, simply because those people live near you and have one head, two ears, and two eyes, just like you. Then time passes and you get to experience college and you make your real friends based on interests, values, and the stuff that matters to you. You're a little embarrassed when you see your former freshman hallmate BFFs during senior week, nearly four years later, right before graduation, because you remember that you used to hang out, and now you don't even say hello to them. It's okay, though, because you see them walking around campus with their real BFFs, and you're happy for them that they found their people, too.

It's almost exactly like that with the mom friends. I hope that all the moms I never connected with have found their people. I am sorry to the ones I ignored, and I forgive those who ignored me. (I know that's something like the Serenity Prayer they say in AA meetings.)

And if anyone wants to wear any kind of version of your kid or anyone else you love or don't love or think is just cool-looking hanging around your neck or from your earlobes or around your wrist, I say go for it. I will not judge, anymore. I have found my mom friends—my real ones.

The Happy Scarf

and Memory

I have a really good memory. I'm often on the receiving end of phone calls, emails, or texts from friends and family members that start with "What was the name of that cute guy from college from that political science class?" or "Where was that place we used to go for dinner in the basement with the couches around the corner from that bar?" Or more challenging ones, like "You know the pretty girl from the movie who's married to the weird-looking guy from that show?" And the thing is, I can usually pull it together on demand for these requests.

Neil and the kids call me the Human Calendar as I recount in great detail our plans from the last seven Labor Day weekends and school vacations. I test myself on past plans, significant dates, and people's names when I can't sleep. I think that's why I majored in history (probably not the most applicable to everyday life) in college, but I thoroughly enjoyed it, and it came rather easily to me. It's all in my memory.

I rely on this memory of mine to relive happy moments from my past, and when I want to, or perhaps need to, I call up those recollections to the instant replay of my mind's eye (very yogic, right?). One such memory is from a cold November day in New York City. It was 2003. My son was a brand-new two-month-old baby, and I left him at home with a brand-new babysitter so that I could spend the day with my mother, shopping for a dress for my brother Jonny's upcoming wedding. It would turn out to be my mother's last November and her last day in New York. I didn't know that then, or maybe I did and I chose not to know it. Memory is a funny thing that way.

My mother and I were on a mission to find me an appropriate sister-of-the-groom dress for my postpartum body. My stomach was not yet completely flat again, and neither was my chest. You can't have it all at once. As I think about the planning of that day now, almost fifteen years later, I've come to realize that my mother and I were really on a mission to spend the day together—to have time that would become a memory, and to make it a happy one. We could have looked for a dress closer to home, or online (secure sites only, obviously), or I could have gone shopping without her. But I didn't. We didn't.

My mother fought through the nausea and fatigue, both side effects from her cancer treatments in the form of targeted chemotherapy injected into her liver, as she rode the train with me to Penn Station on that cold November day. I insisted we take a cab up to Saks Fifth Avenue in midtown, in lieu of our usual subway ride, blaming it on the low temperatures and crowded city while knowing full well that my mother couldn't handle the steps up and down to the subway tracks.

We were successful at Saks. We picked out a black lace Monique Lhuillier dress with a light pink satin ribbon that tied around the waist for me. Back then, Monique Lhuillier was an up-and-coming designer we had never heard of. I think my mother would have gotten a kick out of learning how well known the French-Filipina designer later became. I think of my mom whenever I see a Monique Lhuillier dress in a fashion magazine or on television on a red carpet, which is fairly often. We would have laughed with each other, insisting that we discovered the now famous and very talented dress designer, just as we claimed to discover the strapless wedding gown at Vera Wang when shopping for my own wedding dress, the cupcake cake at the Cupcake Café, and the actor Mark Ruffalo at an off-Broadway play many years prior to then.

We could have gone home that cold day in New York City right after discovering our new favorite dress designer, but we didn't. My mother insisted on having lunch together at Saks and then on walking around "just a few more blocks," as she said to me, to see if we could "find something else." I was a little suspicious. I could tell that she was tired and not feeling great. She sat for longer than usual in the "mother chair" inside the oversize, fancy dressing room on the fancy-dress floor at Saks, and she needed my help to stand up. I saw her pop a few extra antinausea pills that morning, even though she tried to be discreet about it. I agreed to venture on that day, although I wasn't exactly sure why. Common sense told me to get her home as soon as possible, but something else told me to stay—to make the day last longer.

I can still feel my mother's tiny, soft, well-manicured hand in mine as we crossed Fifty-Seventh Street to head into the Burberry flagship store after a long and slow walk up from Saks on Fifty-First. My mother held my hand more tightly that day, much like I did with her hand when I was a child and we crossed that very same street together. I felt very much like her protector on that day—shielding her from the cold, the traffic, and what I knew deep down but didn't want to believe was the inevitable.

We walked into Burberry, and my mother went right over to the cashmere-scarf counter. She asked a nice-looking saleslady to show her the Happy Scarf in light pink. It was similar to the one she wore that day, only hers was hot pink. She pointed that out to the saleslady, who smiled more when my mother spoke to her and, I'm pretty sure, winked at her. The scarf is actually called the Happy Scarf. I swear.

My mother wrapped it around my neck, placing it just so as the fringe fell right below my chin. It felt so soft and cozy—like a warm hug around my neck. I smiled, my mother smiled back, and then she asked the sales lady/her new BFF to remove the tags so that I could wear the new scarf right out of the store.

My mother knew I loved her Happy Scarf, and she wanted me to have one of my own. It was a bit unusual for her to make such a generous purchase out of nowhere and not for any particular occasion. I thanked her and didn't ask any questions. I didn't want to know why she was feeling so generous or why she insisted on shopping more for me when she was so tired, nauseated, and weak.

Of course, I get it now. My mother wanted me to have the scarf. She wanted me to have the dress. She wanted me to have the day, to have the memory. And now I do. I remember almost every moment of that day. I remember how nervous I was helping her in and out of the cabs, how pleased she looked when she saw me in the dress, how she pushed around the food on her plate, hoping I wouldn't notice how little appetite she had, how focused she was on finding me the Happy Scarf, and how happy she was when I told her how much I loved it.

I still love the scarf, and I still wear it now, all these years later. It still makes me happy, even though I didn't think it would. I thought I would never wear it again when she died just a few months after she bought it for me. I thought it would make me sad. I thought everything about her would. That is so not the case. When I wear the scarf, and I wear it a lot, I think of her and the happy times we shared together—not just on that day but on countless days. Of course I wish I had more days with her, but I am so happy I had the ones I did.

I have this running joke with a few close friends of mine when they complain to me about their own, alive mothers or when they recount one of their mother-daughter arguments.

"I am so lucky I don't have to deal with that," I say to them, quite obviously sarcastically. I think some of my friends used to tread lightly on the topic of mothers, whether good or bad, soon after my mom died. They didn't want to upset me or make me jealous or sad. I get that. I respect that. I wouldn't complain to a friend who's trying to get pregnant about the sleepless nights I had with my own babies. But I also like to keep it real. I like to put it all out on the table and talk about it and analyze it until I feel like I might throw up. Neil knows this. He has fallen asleep during many of my long analyses/slowly beating-an-issue-to-death discussions with myself.

My friends know now that they can talk to me about anything, even their mothers—the bad stuff and the good stuff. Their mothers are parts of their lives, and I am a part of theirs, and so I want to know. And yes, I envy my friends when I see them with their mothers. How could I not?

I've come a long way, though, since the days when I closed elevator doors on random mothers and daughters shopping together arm in arm in department stores. "Sorry," I'd say, in my best dumb-girl voice, as I violently pushed the DOOR CLOSE button with my thumb. "I'm trying to keep the door open, but it won't work."

I have gotten to know some of my friends' mothers really well. Some I already knew before my mother died, from growing up or from college. Some have become surrogate mothers for me in many ways. But I know they are not my mothers, and that is okay.

I had my mother. She was a wonderful mother. She had so many amazing qualities, and she taught me so much. She was not perfect, and I'm happy to share those stories with my friends, too, when they start complaining about their alive mothers. I think that made them uncomfortable at first, but I told them how I never wanted to put my mother on a pedestal. She is dead, but she does not need to be anointed with sainthood status.

I still have a lot of questions for my mother, which I know will remain unanswered. But I also have a lot of memories of her. So many of them are happy, and they still make me so happy all these years later.

I am so glad she bought me the Happy Scarf on that cold November day. I am so happy it still makes me happy when I wear it. I think it would make her happy, too.

I Wish Headbands

Didn't Hurt My Head

I love headbands. I always have. I love how they add structure to my face but still allow me to wear my hair down. I think they look good on me. I don't have the cheekbones to pull off a high, fancy ponytail every day, but headbands, I can pull off. I wore them a lot when I was a kid.

I had the everyday ones made of plastic in a rainbow array of colors—the ones with the built-in little combs that attach to your hair as you put them in. I also had the fancier versions for special occasions—the ones covered with grosgrain ribbon, with the bows on the side. I even had some velvet ones. I wore a red velvet headband with a red velvet bow on the side to my bat mitzvah. It went with my long, red-and-pink-flowered corduroy Laura Ashley dress. My mother went to her grave insisting that I was the only girl ever to have worn a Laura Ashley dress to her bat mitzvah. At the time, I was embarrassed by the mole-girl/prairie-bat-mitzvah-girl look, but I'm a little proud of it today when I see thirteen-year-old girls dressed like hookers reading from the Torah up on the bimah at their own bat mitzvahs.

I wore headbands through my teenage years and even into early adulthood. Neil always told me I looked cute when I wore a headband. But here's the thing: Headbands hurt my head, a lot. They've always hurt my head, especially the plastic drugstore kind I used to wear all the time when I was a kid. I'd come home from school with a full-on headband headache, and my mother would say, "Just take the headband off. Don't wear them anymore if they hurt your head so much." I couldn't give in to the reality of the pain of the Goody pink plastic headband or the red velvet Laura Ashley one. I felt a bit like my brain was being squished between my ears the entire day of my bat mitzvah, but everyone said to me "You look so pretty in a headband."

I started wearing those soft headbands made of fabric that go all the way around your head, thinking they wouldn't dig into my head so hard, but they still hurt. I think I have a really big head. Neil tells me I do when I borrow a baseball hat of his and don't have to change his setting on it to make it fit. I lasted about a year with all-the-way-around-your-head athletic headbands.

I don't wear headbands anymore. I don't wear them because they hurt my head. Sounds like kind of simple cause-and-effect stuff, and you'd think I would have given them up a long time ago, but I didn't. Maybe I wasn't ready to. When I go into a lululemon store to buy yoga tops these days, I look longingly at the adorable wraparound headbands that I won't buy for myself anymore.

I wish headbands didn't hurt my head. I really do.

I wish a lot of things: I wish I had a bigger chest. I wish I didn't get a giant pimple on my chin almost every month exactly two days before I get my period. I wish I didn't have to color my prematurely gray hair. I wish I could eat garlic without having a massive stomachache, and I wish I could drink red wine without getting an even more massive headache the next day. I wish they sold Swedish fish in just red-and-orange variety packs, and I wish white chocolate were more readily available than it is now at CVS.

I wish that people of the world could have more time to plan for natural disasters. I wish natural disasters weren't a thing. I wish that religion didn't cause such strife, unrest, and war. I wish that people didn't go hungry, that poverty and racism and abuse in all their forms were things of the past. I wish that people showed more empathy.

I wish that the good guys could always win and that the bad guys would learn how to be better guys (and gals— obviously). I wish that everyone would love what they do and that all people had access to the kinds of education that would allow them to figure out what they want to do and give them the skills they need to do that and the skills they need to make the world a better place.

I wish I could spend more time with my friends and family members whom I don't get to see as much as I'd like to. I wish that they knew that I think of them and wish them only good thoughts when they need it most. I wish that the people I love whom I have wronged know that I am truly sorry for having done wrong to them in the past.

I wish that I could tell my kids that everything will always turn out okay and really mean it. I wish that I could protect them from all the shit in the world that it is impossible to protect them from. I wish I could somehow explain to Neil how lucky I feel that he chose me and I chose him and how comforting it feels to know that there is someone else in my house who has my kids' best interests at heart, too. I wish he would empty the dishwasher without my having to ask him to empty it. I wish that I weren't so scared to take the trash out down our long, dark driveway at night in the winter when he's out of town. I wish I weren't so scared of flying and of driving over the George Washington Bridge by myself and of getting sick and of losing people I love.

I wish my mom had never gotten cancer. I wish she had never died. I wish I could call her up on her cell phone (I still know the number by heart) and ask her how she thinks I'm doing as a mom, a daughter, a sister, a wife, a human being. I wish I could get in an argument with her in real life and then call her back and tell her that I'm sorry. I wish that I hadn't become so damn self-actualized after she died.

I sometimes wonder if I would have become a writer, or gotten into yoga, or became the kind of mother or daughter or friend or sister or person I did if she hadn't died. I don't know. I don't know if it helps to wonder about those things, either.

I wish I didn't wish so much.

My daughter loves headbands, too. They look way cuter on her than they ever did on me. She mostly wears the athletic kind that go all the way around her head. I gave her my old ones and bought her some really cute new ones at lululemon and Athleta. She wears them a lot. They don't hurt her head at all.

I am so glad they don't. But if they do, I wish that she knows that it's okay to take them off, and I wish that she takes them off.

That feels like a pretty good wish to make.

Acknowledgments

ℭℴℭ

This is the book that I've had in me for as long as I can remember. It just took me a while to get it out. There are so many people who have helped me in this process of getting it out of me and out to the world.

Thank you to my first team of amazing readers, not to mention amazing friends—Liza Cohen, Kara Goldman, Nancy Green, Melanie Kaplan, Jill Levitt, Stacey Namm Levine, Amanda Rowley, Penny Schildkraut, Tracy Shedroff, and Lauren Solotoff Stern. Thank you for approving the parts you were in, for being in them in the first place, and for cheering me on along the way.

Thank you to Andrea Jarrell for telling me about She Writes Press and for encouraging me to pursue working with them. Thank you to Amy Blumenfeld for answering every question I had no matter how big or small.

Thank you to the wonderful people at She Writes, most especially Brooke Warner and Samantha Strom. You are true visionaries, and I couldn't have hoped for a better publishing team. Thank you to Annie Tucker for your edits and for your encouragement. You make me look so much better.

Thank you to Tim McGrath for making the items in my jewelry box and my closet come to life in your beautiful sketches in this book exactly as I imagined they could.

Thank you to Crystal Patriarche at BookSparks for being even more excited about promotion than I am, for your amazing publicity ideas, and for making them happen. Thank you to Maggie Ruf for designing the website of my dreams. Thank you to Corinne Strauss for making me look good in just the right light.

Thank you to each and every one of the members of my large, extended, yet closely knit and constantly checking-up-on-me family. That includes all of the cousins and cousin-in-laws, the aunts and uncles who became surrogate parents to me and the real parents too. That includes my beautiful mom who I know is and always will be with me no matter what I am wearing or how I am accessorizing. Thank you to my endlessly curious brother and also my ever-optimistic dad who kind of became my mom and then chose an awesome fake wife to become my fake stepmom, or as she calls herself, my mother in law. And thank you to my real in-laws who read everything I write and also raised a pretty great son.

Thank you to my husband, Neil Lesser, who has been described to me in so many ways—the salt of the earth, the wonder boy, the nice redheaded fellow. You make it all possible, all fun, and all worth it.

And to my kids—Joey and Rebecca Lesser—the pudding, the proof of it all. I don't think you will ever know how happy/lucky/grateful I feel each and every day that I get to be your mom.

About the Author

Rachel Levy Lesser's articles and essays have appeared in various outlets, including *The Huffington Post*, Glamour.com, Parenting.com, *Kveller, Modern Loss, Scary Mommy*, and *The Philadelphia Jewish Exponent*. She is a graduate of The University of Pennsylvania and received her MBA from the Ross School of Business at The University of Michigan. In her previous life as a marketing professional, she worked on the business side of Time Inc. on magazines including *InStyle, Life, People, Real Simple*, and *Sports Illustrated for Kids*. Lesser lives in Pennsylvania with her husband and two children. This is her fourth book.

Selected Titles From *She Writes Press*

She Writes Press is an independent publishing company founded to serve women writers everywhere. Visit us at www.shewritespress.com.

Green Nails and Other Acts of Rebellion: Life After Loss by Elaine Soloway. $16.95, 978-1-63152-919-1. An honest, often humorous account of the joys and pains of caregiving for a loved one with a debilitating illness.

Filling Her Shoes: Memoir of an Inherited Family by Betsy Graziani Fasbinder. $16.95, 978-1-63152-198-0. A "sweet-bitter" story of how, with tenderness as their guide, a family formed in the wake of loss and learned that joy and grief can be entwined cohabitants in our lives.

A Different Kind of Same: A Memoir by Kelley Clink. $16.95, 978-1-63152-999-3. Several years before Kelley Clink's brother hanged himself, she attempted suicide by overdose. In the aftermath of his death, she traces the evolution of both their illnesses, and wonders: If he couldn't make it, what hope is there for her?

Rethinking Possible: A Memoir of Resilience by Rebecca Faye Smith Galli. $16.95, 978-1-63152-220-8. After her brother's devastatingly young death tears her world apart, Becky Galli embarks upon a quest to recreate the sense of family she's lost—and learns about healing and the transformational power of love over loss along the way.

Being Ana: A Memoir of Anorexia Nervosa by Shani Raviv. $16.95, 978-1631521393. In this fast-paced coming-of-age story, Raviv, spirals into anorexia as a misfit fourteen-year-old and spends the next ten years being "Ana" (as many anorexics call it)—until she finally faces the rude awakening that if she doesn't slow down, break her denial, and seek help, she will starve to death.

Don't Leave Yet: How My Mother's Alzheimer's Opened My Heart by Constance Hanstedt. $16.95, 978-1-63152-952-8. The chronicle of Hanstedt's journey toward independence, self-assurance, and connectedness as she cares for her mother, who is rapidly losing her own identity to the early stage of Alzheimer's.